52 Weeks *of*
Conscious Contact

———➤●◄———

52 Weeks *of* Conscious Contact

*Meditations
for Connecting with God,
Self & Others*

MELODY BEATTIE

 HAZELDEN®

Hazelden
Center City, Minnesota 55012-0176

1-800-328-0094
1-651-213-4590 (Fax)
www.hazelden.org

ISBN 13: 978-1-56838-880-9

07 06   6 5 4 3

Cover design by David Spohn
Interior design by Kinne Design
Typesetting by Kinne Design

Editor's note

The stories in this book are based on actual experiences. In some
cases, the names and details have been changed to protect the
privacy of the people involved.

The Twelve Steps of Alcoholics Anonymous are reprinted
with permission of Alcoholics Anonymous World Services,
Inc. (AAWS). AAWS' permission to reprint the Twelve Steps
does not mean that AAWS has reviewed or approved the contents
of this publication, or that AAWS necessarily agrees with the
views expressed therein. Alcoholics Anonymous is a program of
recovery from alcoholism *only*—use of AA's Twelve Steps in connection with programs and activities which are patterned after
AA, but which address other problems, or in any other non-AA
context, does not imply otherwise.

For drama addicts

CONTENTS

CONTENTS

CONTENTS

INTRODUCTION

"What's the name of that place?" I asked my friend. "I can't think of the name of it, but I know you know what I'm talking about."

"What place?"

"It's that place you get to when you're taking care of yourself and trusting God—when everything is all right, even the hard, painful stuff. But it's more than taking care of yourself. That's cold. The place I'm talking about is warmer than that. A place where you're not childish, but where you're innocent—like a child. The world comes alive for you. It's a magical place," I said.

"Maybe that's the name of it," she said. "A magical place."

"Nope, that's too hokey," I said. "It's more than that. Maybe it's what some people call the Kingdom of Heaven?"

"Don't some people call it Nirvana?" she asked. "No. Too many people think you don't go there until after you die."

"I didn't even know about it when I first started taking care of myself," I said. "I found it later, years later, but I know other people know about it too."

Although we never agreed on the name of that place, this is a book about finding it. This book is less a meditation book, and more a book about acquiring and practicing simple life values that will help us get there.

The impetus for this book came from Alcoholic Anonymous's Step Eleven: "Sought through prayer and meditation to improve our conscious contact with God *as we understood Him,* praying only for knowledge of His will for us and the power to carry that out."

Conscious contact is that place many of us have known, but it can be elusive. Sustaining conscious contact seems to require a curious balance between working hard and letting go.

Each week we'll look at one idea, or value, drawn from the well of religions and recovery programs such as Alcoholics Anonymous and Al-Anon. Then we'll explore ways of consciously putting that value into practice throughout the week.

You could read the entire weekly section on one day, apply the ideas throughout the week, and review your progress at week's end. Or, if you prefer daily readings, you could read one of each week's seven sections: a value, an application, a challenge, an inventory focus, an action, a gratitude focus, and, finally, a prayer.

You could progress through the year following the course of the book. Or you could find the weekly topic that applies to a current situation and work on that.

This book is for people who want to do more than let life happen to them.

It's for recovering drug addicts; alcoholics; codependents; people not addicted to anything; people in grief; people just a little on the obsessive side; people who attend church, temple, or synagogue; and people who don't.

This book is for all of us who thought we could skim lightly over the surface of life—who then discovered that's not what we wanted after all. The gifts are below the surface. Have fun uncovering them.

The Quest

1/17/2021

⟿ Day 1 ⟿

Have you ever gone on a scavenger hunt or a treasure hunt? You have a list of things you're looking for, and it's up to you to get creative and find them. Let's pretend that you're on a treasure hunt. Only it's not pretend, it's real.

In the introduction, we talked about that nameless place that many of us are trying to get to, whether we know it or not. The treasures we're seeking are the values we acquire, and through practice, we create this magical place.

I didn't start a formal spiritual quest for values because I wanted to. I started looking for and practicing many of my values because I had to. It was a do-or-die situation.

I started praying because I was killing myself with alcohol and drugs and I couldn't stop drinking on my own. I needed help.

I started learning about the value of living one day at a time because I found myself in such painful, overwhelming circumstances that there was no other way to survive.

Most of my values resulted from painful or uncomfortable situations that demanded that I do something different. Sometimes in my quest for another treasure—improving myself, getting a better job, or improving a relationship—I discovered other treasures such as patience, faith, discipline, guidance, surrender, and service. Over time, I learned that these values were more than emergency-care procedures. Living with these values was a good way to live.

On one of my expeditions, I found myself on top of a famous holy mountain in China. I looked around at the people like myself who had forged their way to the top. Some of them were tourists. They had cameras around their necks. They looked like they were there to see the sights. Any difficulties they encountered on the way to the top were just irritating inconveniences.

Others were more spiritually inclined. They considered each hardship a chance to prove their devotion to spiritual principles. They had humbled themselves by prostrating each step of the way. The trip was a pilgrimage.

Each step was holy and valuable. Whether you call it a quest, a process, a scavenger hunt, a treasure hunt, or a pilgrimage, like Ken Blanchard says, "The only thing that will keep you going is a huge amount of faith and trust in the journey."

Value: This week we will focus on valuing the pilgrimage and the lessons put before us.

༄ Day 2 ༅

"It was the hardest two years of my life," a woman said. "So many painful, unexpected events happened. I felt so abandoned, so lost. I didn't understand what was happening, and I felt tortured by God and life. I didn't think it would ever end. But it did. Now I can look back on that time and say, 'Wow. Look at all I learned. There's nothing that life can bring my way that I can't handle and get through.'"

She learned self-confidence. But whether she's conscious of it or not, this woman is beginning to learn the value of trusting the process.

Application: Sometimes we don't know what we're learning, or whether we're learning anything at all. It's easy to look back on a situation—once it has worked itself out—and be in awe of the process and all that we learned. The time we most need to trust the journey is when it looks like we can't.

✧ Day 3 ✧

Life brings us to our knees. We can't take *it* anymore, whatever *it* is. In desperation, we begin learning new values and living them in new ways, such as prayer, meditation, or service.

Or we're desperate to reach a goal in our lives: more money, a better job, a change in ourselves. So we begin living new values in order to move closer to desirable changes.

For whatever reasons, we begin living by values that work. These values shift our lives. We begin to experience peace and joy. And some of the things we want begin to take place. The pain subsides. The relationship problem improves. We get the new job. The situation becomes better.

Then we relax our practice or attach our happiness to the outcome—the external things—forgetting that it was by living these values that we produced our joy.

Challenge: The hardest thing about values is remembering that they are the real treasures.

ᴄᴀ **Day 4** ᴀᴠ

Some problems are slow-burners. We live with them for a long time and get used to mucking about in them.

Other problems strike hard and fast, coming down on us like a hailstorm.

It can be difficult, when the storm hits, to remember that the journey is a benevolent and holy one, a process that is working with us to help us learn something new.

> ***Inventory Focus:*** *Are you going through a situation right now that feels torturous, like it's happening for no reason other than to irritate or punish you? Can you believe, just a little, that what you're going through right now is a valuable part of your life and that an overall benevolent process is taking place? Can you at least believe that this situation has the possibility of shaping you in valuable ways and bringing gifts to your life?*

ᴄᴀ **Day 5** ᴀᴠ

A recent article suggested that the biggest cause of stress is the frustration of not getting what we want. We can reduce our stress by turning frustration into fascination.

> ***Action:*** *Instead of asking, "Why is this happening to me?" ask, "What am I learning now?"*

ᴄᴀ **Day 6** ᴀᴠ

I was walking through my house stomping my feet and whining about a seemingly impossible problem I was facing. That's when I remembered that stomping my feet, whining, and resisting will not solve the problem. It will not make it go away. Practicing my values will.

Gratitude Focus: *This week, we can practice gratitude for the lesson we're learning right now, whether or not we understand it yet. Sometimes the best teachers are tough circumstances. We can be grateful for those teachers too.*

✥ Day 7 ✥

The fog lifts. The way becomes clear. It is with sheer joy that we realize we're not alone. Something valuable and important was being worked out. However difficult that process, it changed us, transformed us, took us to a new place.

"Next time," we think, "I won't ride that extra roller coaster of emotion caused by not trusting the process. I'll trust it all along."

Prayer: *Higher Power, help me remember that you're not torturing me, you're teaching me. Please show me—in a way I can understand—what you want me to learn. Help me remember that practicing the values I'm learning is the true source of joy. Guide and bless me in my pilgrimage through the year.*

Integrity

～ Day 1 ～

I heard the water pipes gushing under the house. I was so busy. A busted pipe was the last thing I needed. Whether it was what I needed or not, it was what I had. The high tide frequently banged against the exposed plumbing. Calling the plumber for a quick repair job was part of my duties as condominium president and manager.

I called directory assistance for the number for the local plumber, then I called the plumber. An hour later, two men in plumbing uniforms showed up at the door. I explained the problem. They said they'd get right to it. I went back to work.

An hour later, they pounded on the door again. This time they were scowling.

"You'd better come look," one of the men said.

I had dealt with these plumbers time and time again. I trusted them.

"Just fix it, please," I said. "I'm busy."

Another hour passed. They knocked on the door again. This time, they insisted I come with them.

"What is the problem?" I asked.

They shook their heads, looking concerned. "We can't repair the pipe that broke," they said. "The fittings are corroded. It's bad," they said. "You're going to have to replace all the plumbing under the house."

"Just tell me the bottom line," I said. "How much is it going to cost."

"Somewhere between five and seven thousand dollars."

Now they had my attention. "Show me," I said.

I went under the house with them. What had previously been a dripping pipe was now a rain shower under the house.

Then, a light went on. There were two plumbing companies by the same name that serviced the area. One was a highly reputable plumber, the one I called all the time. The other by the same name wasn't.

"Which plumbing company are you with?" I asked. They explained they were *the other one.* Directory assistance had connected me with the wrong one.

I said they needed to leave immediately. They said they needed to be paid for the time they had worked. I said they hadn't finished the job. They said it would cost me thousands of dollars for them to complete the work. We were at a standoff. For just a moment, I considered going ahead. After all, I was already into these guys for some money. "Maybe I'll let them finish the job," I thought.

Then I remembered, "Don't dance with the devil."

"Let's negotiate," I said. "I'm going to give you something, but you're not going to get what you want because I didn't get what I want." After some haggling, I paid them a small amount of money and they left.

I called the other plumber. In two hours, the job was properly done. The bill was $87.50.

Encountering integrity can be like a breath of fresh air.

A person of integrity has honorable intentions, is trust-worthy, and is honest. An air of high drama or manipulation does not surround acts of integrity. Acts of integrity stand on their own.

Value: This week we'll explore the value of integrity—other people's and our own.

◈ Day 2 ◈

Some people just can't help themselves; they simply lack integrity. We, too, can lapse into less than honorable behavior at times. The burden, then, is on us to take steps to protect ourselves from other people's lack of integrity, and from our own.

Application: Whenever our guts go off because we don't trust someone, or whenever we're in a state of high anxiety because we're not living up to our own standards for ourselves, it's time to get back to basics. That's when it's time to quickly assess which of our own values are needed to get us back on track.

◈ Day 3 ◈

A friend had gone to work for an employer with a reputation for dishonesty. Then he wondered, in the end, why that employer lied, conned, and screwed over him. Story's not over. He ran into the employer years later and got mixed up with him again.

"I was trying to make him be honest with me. I was insisting that he treat me fairly this time." We all know the ending. He got screwed over again.

Dancing with the devil is seductive—in work and in

love. It's an enticing challenge; we want to make somebody change, treat us right, and give us what we know we deserve. Not living up to our own values can be seductive too. "This situation is an exception," we think. "This time, the values I believe in don't really apply."

It's easy to look around at the world and think that the only ones who really make it are the people who lie, cheat, and steal. Or we see something we really want, and we believe we can't get it honestly, so we set our values aside for a time.

Acknowledging other people's lack of integrity usually hurts. At least it stings. By the time we see it, we may be in over our head. "I'll just keep dealing with this person," we think. "Try and recoup my losses so I don't lose any more."

I'm as prone to dancing with the devil as anyone else. We pay a price each time we do.

Challenge: The hardest part about living with values can be simple pride. It's hard to admit that we got conned. It can be humiliating to admit that we can't have what we want, or that we've not lived up to our values, or that we have a lesson to learn because we made a mistake. Here's a hint: Learn to take your losses and run.

↬ Day 4 ↫

Do you value integrity in others?

Inventory Focus: Are the people you're involved with in business, play, and love living by values that are harmonious with yours? Are you dancing with the devil somewhere in your life, either by associating with people who don't have integrity, or by not living up to your personal values?

ᗕᐤ **Day 5** ᔆᐤ

Play a little game with yourself. Find the value in each situation you find yourself in today.

Action: *You don't live in utopia yet. Forgo naïveté. Protect yourself when others display a lack of integrity. Work on living by your values.*

ᗕᐤ **Day 6** ᔆᐤ

I'm not sure whether experience is the best teacher, but it's a consistent one.

Gratitude Focus: *We can be grateful for all the situations that teach us the value of integrity. We can be grateful for all the opportunities we have to practice our values each day.*

ᗕᐤ **Day 7** ᔆᐤ

When we can't control anything or anyone around us, we can gain a sense of control by living with integrity. Figure out what you need to do to take care of yourself. Don't judge others too harshly for not living up to your values, and give yourself a break for being imperfect. Then let God handle the rest.

Prayer: *Grant me the courage to change the things I can, and the presence of mind to know when someone is acting without integrity toward me. Help us acquire a treasure chest of the real gems in life—the values we acquire and live by each day.*

Practice

☙ Day 1 ❧

When I began studying martial arts, I felt awkward about the moves I was learning. "Can't you give me a book?" I asked my instructor. "I need a set of rules to tell me exactly how to do this, so I know when I'm getting it right."

"You don't need to read a book," he said. "Keep practicing. You may not always know when you're doing it wrong, but you'll know when you get it right."

Applying the appropriate value to a given situation requires practice. Sometimes we need to practice patience in a particular relationship. On the other hand, there is a point when we need to practice setting a boundary and saying, "That's enough and that's it." When do we need to let go a little more, and when have we let go too much?

Some situations require us to express our feelings, like anger or sadness. At what point, however, have we mucked about in our upset feelings too long, refusing to forgive someone? When is tolerance the life-giving value of the day, and when have we tolerated enough?

What about prayer and faith? How much time do we spend on our knees or with hands folded, talking to God? On the other hand, when do we get up and go do something ourselves—take an appropriate action to help change our own lives?

How about using intuition? When do we rely on what feels right, and when do we use good old rational thought instead?

There are no hard and fast rules in life for which values to apply and when. Calling on our personal values can be puzzling and confusing. And we may do a lot of our learning by trial and error. Learning which value to apply can feel like hit and miss.

Most of the time, I'm not learning what I think I'm learning anyway. Something different is taking place, something deeper. It's as if the universe gives us something to occupy what writer Natalie Goldberg calls "the monkey mind" so we can move forward along our path.

Just keep practicing the values you know. Stay open to learning something new. Practice might not make us perfect, but it will help us progress along our path. And in any situation we find ourselves, it'll give us something beneficial to do.

Value: This week we'll explore the consistent practice of the values we find meaningful in our lives. When we focus on our values, we improve the quality of our daily lives, and when we encounter a challenge, we'll have a better idea of what value to apply.

✑ Day 2 ✑

Keep throwing values at the problem. Eventually something will stick.

Application: Consider each day of your life as an opportunity to consciously learn, practice, or apply values that are important to you. Usually the situations that most require us to practice our values feel the most difficult.

ᔟᕈ **Day 3** ᕈᔟ

It's easy to become lazy and complacent, but living our values requires daily practice. It's also tempting to compartmentalize our lives. "Oh, I believe in values like honesty and surrender," we say, "but this part of my life is immune." Or it doesn't occur to us that principles like powerlessness, turning a struggle over to a Higher Power, and praying for God's Will for us might work in financial, work, and relationship problems.

> **Challenge:** *The biggest challenge to consistently practicing values is this: We have to stop luxuriating in being victims and take responsibility for ourselves. Practicing values means the ball is always in our court.*

ᔟᕈ **Day 4** ᕈᔟ

When my son died, I didn't want to play the game anymore. His death broke every rule I thought was important. His death hurt my trust—not my faith—in God. It wasn't that I didn't believe in God anymore. I absolutely believed in God, but I also related to the words of C. S. Lewis: "So this is what God is really like."

We're all in the game, whether we like it or not. It's a game called *cause and effect*. If we don't play by the rules— live by values—we're going to reap the consequences of living that way. We may have been hurt by life, but not practicing our values hurts other people, and it hurts us.

> **Inventory Focus:** *If you are recovering from alcoholism or addiction, are you attending meetings and working the Steps? If codependency issues are a problem, are you paying attention to them in recovery? If you're not*

addicted and not codependent, do you have any formal or informal regular practice to help yourself stay spiritually in shape and on track?

✎ **Day 5** ✎

It happened in my first year or two of sobriety. The old part of me took over, and I couldn't think of one good reason in the world not to drink. I called a sponsor, a mentor in the program.

"You're powerless over alcohol, and if you drink, your life becomes unmanageable," said my sponsor, paraphrasing the First Step of Alcoholics Anonymous. "If you drink, you may either die, go to jail, or go insane. How's that for a reason not to drink?"

"That's a good enough reason for me," I said.

Sometimes practicing a value means taking only a moment of our time to focus on that truth.

Action: You don't have to overwhelm or overexert yourself. You don't have to become fanatical or go to extremes. But instead of always allowing your thoughts and behaviors to be spontaneous and random, why not, at least occasionally, consciously focus on and practice a value instead?

✎ **Day 6** ✎

When I first started learning about values like letting go, expressing my feelings honestly, and surrendering, I thought, "Oh, how nice. This was the lesson. I'll just apply it to this circumstance, and go merrily on my way." I have long since discovered that living these values is not a once-in-a-while thing. It has taken me a long time to understand—to really get—that most life experiences are not a one-time lesson. We're going to need to practice our values all our lives.

Gratitude Focus: *Just starting out on a spiritual path? New to recovery? Been at it for a long time? We can be grateful that no matter how long we've been striving to apply spiritual principles in our lives, the basics always work.*

༽ **Day 7** ༼

Practice a value that applies to a life problem right now. Do the best you can. You don't have to do it perfectly. That's why we call it *practice*. Our values will stand on their own.

Prayer: *Please help me develop confidence in you, in myself, and in the principles that I am learning. Show me how well these values work.*

Challenges

ᘓ Day 1 ᘍ

I used to think challenges were bad. My thinking has turned around on that.

Did you ever try to do something that was so easy, so piece-of-cake, so guaranteed that you didn't have one emotion, doubt, or fear about it? Boring, isn't it?

"Oh my God," I thought. "How am I ever going to find my way through this? If I don't figure this out, I'll die. Or go to jail. Dear God, please help me." The fear, anxiety, and sheer importance and improbability I faced when I first got sober both overwhelmed and motivated me to stay sober. All of it pushed me to search for answers, to get up off my butt and go to meetings, to ask for help, to be of service.

Challenges get our attention in a world where that's often hard to do.

"What is this? What's happened to me? I'm sinking in quicksand," I thought when I began to face my codependency issues. The confusion, fear, and anger felt uncomfortable enough to motivate me to change.

The same was true about the challenge of being a single parent, after my divorce. The sheer terror of being faced with the sole responsibility for raising two children was both too much and just what I needed to get my attention and help direct me to the next set of lessons in life. The challenges of single parenthood brought out my best.

When my son died, the challenge became too much. This time, I didn't bounce back. But eventually, just the teeniest part of me became curious about where something this devastating might lead.

Even the small challenges—those problems that interrupt our day or our mood—can serve to get our attention. If we are mindful, we can find positive motivators in small problems.

"Why didn't anyone tell me how hard this was going to be?" I've heard many people express these kinds of fears about sobriety, recovery from codependency, parenthood, life. I've said it myself. Remember, it takes heat and pressure to turn carbon into diamonds. The pressure of challenges is what shapes and forms us.

Value: This week we'll explore the value of a genuine rise-to-the-occasion, feet-to-the-fire, step-up-to-the-plate challenge.

∽ Day 2 ∾

We want enough challenge in life to get our attention. With practice, we can turn our fears into determination. Opposition can be our greatest teacher. A good challenge can bring out our best.

Application: Whenever we're wondering why something has to be so hard, it may be time to remember the value of challenges. Whenever we're creating self-sabotaging challenges because we're bored, it's time to examine the value of the challenges we're taking on.

∾ **Day 3** ∾

"My husband and I finally got our financial situation stabilized," a woman said. "We knew where the money was going to come from, and we had enough each month to pay bills. My husband and I both woke up one morning—almost immediately after this happened—and decided we needed to buy a bigger, more expensive house.

"It got right down to the wire. We were in the process of getting the loan when something clicked in me," she said. "Why are we doing this? We're just setting ourselves up to have a challenge to alleviate boredom.

"We backed out of the deal. We didn't need a bigger, more expensive home. What we needed to do was create a positive challenge in our lives, not financially sabotage ourselves."

There's a danger with challenges. Some of us might get so used to needing something to push up against and an occasion to rise to that we begin creating drama-addict challenges, the kind that sabotage our relationships, work, and lives.

"I didn't love the guy. I didn't even like him," a friend said. "But I ended up marrying him—and divorcing him—just because getting him was such a challenge."

Challenges are good. But we need to make sure that responding to a challenge isn't the sole criterion for the decisions we make.

Challenge: *The hardest thing about challenges is determining which ones to take on.*

ᘓ Day 4 ᘗ

I watched a man I know help his wife take care of their babies.

"How did you learn to be such a good dad?" I asked. He explained that his father had been a great dad. His mother had died when he was three, leaving his father on his own to care for him and his baby sister.

"So he just stepped up to the plate?" I asked.

"Like Babe Ruth," he said.

Inventory Focus: What—or who—is challenging you? Are you creating healthy challenges or unnecessary chaos? Do you want it just because you can't have it, or do you really want it? Are you stepping up to the plate and accepting the real challenges in your life?

ᘓ Day 5 ᘗ

"Why did you climb those mountains," someone asked about my trip to China.

"Because they were there," I said.

Action: There's a fine line between having enough challenge that you roll up your sleeves and decide to do your best, and having so much pressure that you cave in.

You can use the energy from legitimate challenges to change, grow, and solve problems. Anger, frustration, and fear can be great motivators. Instead of being over-whelmed, maybe you can try to take an active interest in what you're about to do.

If you are bored, you can create healthy challenges instead of self-sabotaging ones. Set new goals and dreams in relationships, at work, and in your spiritual life. Instead of picking a fight in a relationship, try setting a goal to grow closer to the person you love. Bored at work? Maybe you need to put more of yourself into your job, or learn something new, or change what you're doing.

Most of us need something to push against. It's harder when life's events come out of the blue and push us. It's one thing to be pushed against. It's another to be pushed so hard we fall down and stay there. Maybe you could start getting up, just a little? If your problems have knocked you down, turn problems into challenges. Get back up on your feet and take them on.

ᘓᕽᕽ Day 6 ᕽᕽᘓ

Thank God this world is so interesting.

Gratitude Focus: *We can be grateful for the legitimate challenges in our lives and the way they've shaped and formed us.*

ᘓᕽᕽ Day 7 ᕽᕽᘓ

So it's a little uncomfortable. Stretch. Strain. See what you're capable of?

Prayer: *Show me what I am capable of achieving with your help. Make me who I am meant to be.*

Inventory

ᴄᴍ **Day 1** ᴧᴠ

The first time I took an inventory of myself, it was because I had to. I was in a treatment program. A judge had sentenced me there "for as long as it takes." The treatment staff wasn't going to let me out until I sat down and took a look at myself.

"A searching and fearless moral inventory" is what Step Four of Alcoholics Anonymous recommends. I was overwhelmed by the process. All I saw was this big blur of self. I started writing about one small aspect of myself that I was able to recognize. Within minutes, I saw more. This inventory process took on a life of its own.

What was I aware of about myself that was a problem? What was bugging me most, the thing about myself I least wanted any other human being to know? What was the thing I least wanted to admit to myself? What did I fear and whom did I resent?

We were supposed to also inventory the good qualities about ourselves. I couldn't find any of those.

"You're persistent," the clergy person at treatment said. I hung onto that asset for years. I thought it was my only good quality.

It's an interesting phenomenon—how quick and easy

it is to see qualities we like in other people. It's also a snap to see what we don't like in other people, qualities that we think they should change. Taking other people's inventories is a breeze. Taking our own is hard work.

The year was 1982. My husband at the time wanted to go to Las Vegas. I wanted him to stay home, but I didn't know how to express how I felt. About the third night he was gone, I felt that anxiety in my gut. I knew he was out of control, drinking again. I had a party planned for the next morning. I was throwing an open house for a neighbor graduating from college. Eighty people were due to show up. My husband was supposed to be home to help.

I didn't clean my house. I didn't prepare the food. I sat calling him in Vegas, dialing a number over and over again for eight straight hours. "What he's doing is crazy," I kept thinking. "What he's doing is wrong and nuts."

About ten o'clock that night, I saw the light. "Eighty people are coming to my home tomorrow, and here I sit, dialing a number that will not be answered? He might be out of control," I thought, "but what I'm doing is crazy."

Sometimes we need to take our own inventory to get out of an uncomfortable stuck place, to look at patterns and see what's going on. Other times, looking at our own behaviors gives us the freedom to finally have and live our lives. Taking our own inventory doesn't have to be a big gruesome job—although sometimes it is. Rather, it can be a way to stop pointing our finger at others and take responsibility for ourselves.

Value: Call it taking stock of ourselves or cleaning our side of the street, taking our own inventory is the value this week.

✑ **Day 2** ✑

When all we can see is what other people are doing wrong *to* us, it's time to take the focus off them and put it on ourselves.

> ***Application:*** *Whenever we feel defensive, whenever we find ourselves talking a lot about what others are doing wrong, whenever we'd just as soon not look at ourselves, it's time to do just that.*

✑ **Day 3** ✑

"My boss pulled me aside to tell me about something I was doing wrong," a man shared with me. "But he didn't just critique my work. He criticized everything I did. I walked away without a shred of self-esteem."

Many of us grew up with a lot of criticism. We may live with someone now who's very critical, or we may be highly critical of ourselves. The thought of looking closely at ourselves can make us cringe. We may feel afraid that if we look closely at who we are, we'll be left without self-worth.

The purpose of looking at ourselves isn't to barrage ourselves with criticism. It's to identify behaviors we're doing that are sabotaging ourselves so we can begin the process of change.

Look fearlessly. Look carefully. We can critique what we do without judging who we are. A difficult thing about looking at ourselves fearlessly can be getting past the fear.

> ***Challenge:*** *The hardest part about looking at ourselves can be that, compared to other people, we think every-thing we do looks good. Besides, if we find a defect, then we might need to change.*

◡ Day 4 ◠

What did you do today? What did you like about what you did? What didn't you like, that you'd like to do better tomorrow? See! Answering those questions wasn't that hard. The way we need to inventory ourselves is *fearlessly,* not *brutally.*

> **Inventory Focus:** *Are you willing to be as honest with yourself as you can?*

◡ Day 5 ◠

If we don't take our inventory, sooner or later someone will take it for us.

> **Action:** *Taking a thorough inventory is a good way to get your life on track when you've hit a wall, such as with alcoholism or codependency. An inventory can be helpful when you keep running into the same patterns in any area of your life: work, finances, or relationships.*
>
> *Many people think that taking a few minutes to look at themselves each day is a good maintenance tool. Some people do this by keeping a journal. Others prefer a mental debriefing, or review, at the end of the day.*
>
> *Looking at other people may be fun and easy, but looking at yourself is a powerful thing to do.*

◡ Day 6 ◠

The easiest way to figure out what's bothering me about me is to listen to what I say bothers me about others. Sometimes other people are a better mirror than the one on the wall.

Gratitude Focus: *We can be grateful for all the people who help us feel safe enough to honestly look at who we are and what we do.*

✌ **Day 7** ✍

I was reminiscing one day with a friend about a sage voice in the program of Alcoholics Anonymous, Bill M., a man who sponsored many of us when we first got sober.

"I was sitting and complaining about someone else, about how screwed up they were and what they needed to do to change," my friend said. "Bill M. listened to me carry on. 'You know why we take other people's inventories, don't you?' he finally asked.

" 'No,' I said.

" 'Because our own makes us want to throw up.' "

Let off steam. Don't deny how you really feel. But if you insist on talking about someone's flaws, at least once in a while let them be your own.

Prayer: *Give me the courage to look fearlessly at myself. Help me see my weak spots. Please give me the stamina to keep looking until I find something to feel good about too.*

Power in Action

༦ **Day 1** ໑

Inertia is a powerful force. So is compulsive behavior.

"Insanity is doing the same thing over and over and expecting different results," writer Earnie Larsen has said for years. I think it goes one step further. Insanity is doing the same thing over and over because we can't find the button that says "Stop."

"My mom was dying," a woman said. "I went to live with her, take care of her. We had our issues, like most mothers and daughters. But I love my mom, and this was the end of her life.

"She had a studio apartment. We both lived in that one room. I had to get out of there once in a while. Whenever I returned from being out, I knew what to expect. My mom would slam me with sarcastic remarks. She'd say things like, 'It's nice to know that I'm not as important to you as your friends.'

"My mom had used sarcasm to cover her emotions all my life. I had tried to explain this to her, and how I felt when she was sarcastic with me. I had told her it was okay for her to be vulnerable with me and just say how she really feels. She either didn't get it, or she didn't want to change.

"I had to keep taking breaks. I couldn't be there twenty-four hours a day. But I'd cringe when I came home, dreading her caustic remarks. One night, I tiptoed in. I was praying to God that Mom would be asleep. She wasn't. She was lying there waiting for me to walk through the door.

"I took off my coat. Asked her how she was doing. Said I had a nice night.

"'I'm glad you had a good time,' Mom said. 'But I feel really sad and scared when I'm alone. And I feel better now that you're here.'

"I couldn't believe what I heard. Don't tell me it's too late to do things differently. My mom made a choice and took the action to change in the last week of her life."

Putting values into action in our lives takes courage and hard work. Sometimes the little steps we take mean a lot.

Value: The value this week is taking action to change the things we can.

∾ Day 2 ∾

"Remember the old Chinese handcuffs thing," a friend reminds me when I get stuck doing the same thing over and over, even though whatever I'm doing doesn't work.

A Chinese handcuff is a toy, a small bamboo tube, about four inches long. You stick an index finger in each end. Then when you pull, you're trapped. The harder you pull, the more stuck you get. Your instinctive reaction—not the handcuffs—keeps you trapped. To set yourself free you have to take certain steps. Letting go isn't enough. You have to relax, then gently push in before you can pull yourself loose.

When my friend tells me to remember the Chinese handcuffs thing, he's reminding me that sometimes taking action means relaxing and doing the opposite of what our instincts tell us to do.

***Application:** If we have tried to do something a hundred times, and the way we're doing it hasn't worked, it probably still won't the next time. It may be time to take action and do something else.*

ᵕᕲ Day 3 ᕲᵕ

We all like to feel comfortable. But doing something new, especially taking an action to change, usually doesn't feel comfortable. It feels awkward and strange.

Sometimes depression and anxiety can block us from taking the actions we want and need to take. Not taking these actions can increase our depression and anxiety, and we feel even less motivated to act. This cycle can keep us trapped.

If depression and anxiety are so severe they're stopping you from taking actions to live your life, you may need to seek professional help and get those issues under control. That in itself is taking action.

***Challenge:** The hardest thing about taking positive steps to change can be having enough hope to believe that what we do matters and the steps we take will work.*

ᵕᕲ Day 4 ᕲᵕ

"How do I change?" a woman asked her friend.

"HOW," the friend replied.

"Yes, that's what I'm asking. How do I change?"

"I told you," her friend said. "HOW is how you change. Honesty. Openness. Willingness to try."

HOW isn't new. It's not groundbreaking. But sometimes the best road to take is ground that's been trod.

A friend called one day when I was struggling to take an action in my life that just wasn't coming together. "Are you willing to try?" she asked.

"Right now I'm working on wanting to want to," I said. "That's the best I can do."

Inventory Focus: *Are you willing to take actions, small baby steps, even when those steps feel awkward and uncomfortable? If you're not willing to take action to change, are you at least willing to become willing? That's an action too. Willingness is a prerequisite to receive the power to act.*

༄ Day 5 ༄

Acting as if is another recovery truism that's been around for a long time. I still use it regularly in my life. I know people who are not in recovery—athletes, performers, artists—who use the technique too.

All it means is that if it's time to act, we do—whether taking that action feels comfortable or not. Instead of doing nothing, or waiting for confidence, success, or inspiration to overtake and motivate us first, we go ahead and move forward with an action anyway and let the good feelings catch up to us. We act as if the desired change has already taken place.

Action: *"I didn't pay my bills because I didn't have enough money to pay them off in full," a man told me.*

29

"I had to learn that I could make payments and pay off the whole bill by paying a little at a time."

Sometimes you can sabotage yourself by trying to do too much at once. If you can't stop drinking or using drugs by yourself, are you willing to ask for help? If you can't accept everything about your life in one fell swoop, are you willing to accept where you are and how you feel today? If you can't forgive someone, are you willing to start praying for that person and let go of the resentment you feel?

Break whatever you are trying to do into small steps. Then take the first step first.

৩৯ **Day 6** ৩৯

I've heard it said that we never need to do anything that we won't be given the power and strength to do. That's true. But sometimes to get past our fear and nervousness, we need a little push.

Gratitude Focus: *We can be grateful for all the pushes life gives us to change.*

৩৯ **Day 7** ৩৯

Sometimes I feel as if life is prodding me, poking me, pushing me. It hurts sometimes. But then I think, "Oh, I get it. I'm not supposed to ignore the pain. Pain can motivate me to change."

Prayer: *Guide me into taking the actions you want me to take.*

Gratitude

～ **Day 1** ～

"My relationship is on the rocks. My finances could be a lot better. And this house I live in, well it's the worst. Wouldn't I be happier somewhere else? Let me think, where would that magical place of happiness be? One thing's for sure. It's not where I am."

Can you hear yourself in these words? It is easy to look around and see all that is wrong. Life can be irritating, less than we hoped for, and sometimes it really hurts.

"I want something," a woman said to me one day. "I just don't know what it is. But one thing I do know is I don't have it right now."

"The grass is always greener on the other side" is an old cliché, but it isn't true. The grass right where you are, no matter where that place is, is just as green as it is any-where else. And if it's not green or it's all dried up, maybe it's because you're not watering it enough.

Those moments that surpass our wildest expectations are fleeting and rare. People, places, and circumstances that don't measure up to our hopes abound. Learning to want what you have and be where you are is an art. So is learn-ing how to get to wherever you're going to.

Here's the secret. You're a magician, a wizard. You can

turn present situations into something better. Point your magic wand. Now say "thank you" for everything exactly as it is.

People tell us to count our blessings. The problem is, when we're depressed, we don't feel blessed. Learning an attitude of gratitude takes practice and effort. It's the key to being happy in whatever circumstances we find ourselves in.

Value: Whether we call it a feeling, an attitude, or an action we take, gratitude is the value we'll look at and practice this week.

⟡ Day 2 ⟡

"But you don't know my circumstances. That won't work for me. I don't have it as good as other people. You should see my life. It's a mess."

Religious leaders, psychiatrists, physicists, new and ancient philosophies agree. We don't see things as they are, we see things as we are. When we're restless, irritable, and discontented, everything looks bad. That's because we're practicing negativity. It's a powerful form of magic, only the magic it works is dark.

Practice deliberate gratitude. Force it and fake it if you must. When you look again, after practicing gratitude, you will see that we—and our circumstances—have shifted into a different place.

Application: Got a situation that's bugging us? Don't know how to resolve or even accept the problems in our lives? Whenever we look around and don't like what we see, it's time to say, "Thank you for everything exactly as it is." When we look around and feel blessed, it's time to say thanks too. Let the white magic begin.

ᨘᨘ **Day 3** ᨘᨘ

Gratitude isn't denial. We can practice gratitude without denying how we feel. Sometimes we do need to change the circumstances in our lives. But we usually can't do that until we accept what we have and who we are now.

One challenge about practicing gratitude is that the things we most need to be grateful for are often the things causing us the most misery. Practicing gratitude when we most need to do it can feel like the most unnatural act in the world.

Practicing gratitude can be difficult when we're depressed or going through deep grief. Some things in life are so tragic that we'll never be grateful that the event occurred.

I'm not grateful for my son's death. I'd have him back in a heartbeat if I could. But I'm grateful that I had him in my life. I'm grateful for the lessons I've learned since he died. And I'm grateful I'm happy again.

Challenge: *The hardest thing about practicing gratitude can be surrendering to God and trusting his will.*

ᨘᨘ **Day 4** ᨘᨘ

A friend called in a cynical mood. He was disgusted with his job and his less-than-ideal house.

"I want you to do something," I said. "Practice being grateful for everything you don't like every day, five times a day, for the next month. Force it. Fake it. Do whatever you have to. But you've been practicing misery about these same things for the past three years. That hasn't worked. Why not give gratitude a try?"

He was reluctant. I told him a story from my life. The first house I ever bought was decrepit, falling apart. Holes went clear through to the outside. I didn't know how to fix it up. For the first three months I lived there, I went downstairs each night after putting my daughter to bed, sat in the middle of the ugly living room, and complained and cried. The situation didn't improve. I decided to try something else. I began practicing gratitude instead. I said, "Thank you for this house, the holes in the walls, and the way I feel." *Thank you* became a meditative chant. Over the next nine months, I started fixing up that house, and it turned into the most beautiful home on the block. Thirty years later, I still remember it as my favorite house. Perspective is a strange thing. It wasn't just about transforming that house. Going through that experience gave me an opportunity to see for myself that gratitude works.

My friend was quiet for a while. "I used to practice gratitude," he said. "Then I forgot. Practicing gratitude was how I was able to move out of my last house. It helped change my life. I have to go," he said. "I can't wait to start practicing gratitude again."

Inventory Focus: *Have you been practicing misery? How's that working? Have you learned about the power of gratitude yet? Are you willing to give it a try?*

ᐁᐁ **Day 5** ᐁᐁ

Gratitude isn't a tool to manipulate the universe or God. It's a way to acknowledge our faith that everything happens for a reason even if we don't know what that reason is.

Action: Just say thanks for everything. Make a gratitude box. On slips of paper, write about everything you consider a blessing and everything you feel miserable about. Then regularly take the slips out and thank God for what's on that slip. Or hold the whole box in your hands and be grateful for all of it, all at once.

༜ **Day 6** ༜

Gratitude feeds on itself. It breeds acceptance. It turns what we have into enough, and more.

Gratitude Focus: We can keep saying thank you, even when we don't mean it. Pretty soon we won't have to fake it anymore. It will become a natural heartfelt act.

༜ **Day 7** ༜

See how powerful *thank you* is. The magic isn't somewhere else. It's where you are right now.

Prayer: Thank you for my life.

Prayer

༄ **Day 1** ༄

Did you ever call someone on the phone, thinking they weren't home and expecting to get their answering machine instead? That's how it was the first time I called God.

I was in treatment for chemical dependency. I had been there almost three months, and I still couldn't stop using drugs. I didn't know how. I was ingesting anything I could get my hands on, from an industrial-sized can of nutmeg (I'd heard you can hallucinate with it), to marijuana (not my drug of choice, but it did in a pinch), to the old-fashioned inhaler decongestants (they can be like cheap speed).

I was out of my mind. I had a serious prison sentence hanging over my head for possession of narcotics and some drugstore burglaries. A lot was riding on this treatment. And a dilemma had presented itself. An acquaintance from the streets had just entered the program. He had given me a handful of methamphetamine—my best score yet during treatment. But my probation officer was scheduled to visit me the following morning. I thought I'd just take a little.

I ended up staying up all night, bug-eyed and paranoid

from the speed, wondering if I'd get caught. I made it through the visit with my probation officer the next day without attracting his attention. Even though I escaped getting detected by him, I couldn't run from myself anymore.

After he left, I sat down on my bed. "God, I don't know if you're real or not," I said. "But if you are, and there's a program here that will help me stop using, please help me get it," I said.

Two days later, I was sitting on the lawn smoking a joint. I took a hit, then laid back to stare at the clouds. In that moment, the sky seemed to turn purplish. I knew that I knew—that deepest kind of knowing—that God was real, and I had no right to keep using alcohol and other drugs anymore. "If I put just half as much energy into doing the right thing as I've put into doing the wrong thing, there isn't anything I can't do," I thought. I took one more hit of the joint. Then I went into the treatment center building and threw myself into recovery with all my heart and soul.

Two days later, another acquaintance came through the treatment center. He had some good dope. Did I want some? "No thanks," I said. "I don't get high anymore." I surprised my friend. I surprised myself even more.

I live in California, where celebrities can be seen often. People, including myself, will flock around celebrities, hoping to have just a few words with someone we consider powerful and important. It's fun, but my life has never been improved by getting an autograph or meeting somebody famous. Talking to God has changed my life.

Value: *Prayer is the value this week.*

ᴥ **Day 2** ᴥ

Most of us have heard the phrase "Stick with the winners." Who we associate with can directly influence our thoughts, attitudes, emotions, and behaviors. Why not spend a few minutes a day consciously connecting with God?

> ***Application:*** *Prayer is a good thing to wrap around us every day. Whenever we get in a jam, get confused, need help, or don't know what to do next, taking a minute to talk to God and asking for guidance is a good call.*

ᴥ **Day 3** ᴥ

After I left treatment, praying in the morning became part of my routine. I prayed as though my life depended on it, because it did. I didn't feel like I had begun my day properly unless I started it with a recovery prayer, asking for God's help and guidance.

After my son died, I was so angry about his death that I stopped my morning routine. But there came a time when I had to get back to my routine of talking to God. It can be hard to believe that God cares about the details of our lives. It can feel awkward talking to a force we can't see or hear.

> ***Challenge:*** *For me, the hardest thing about praying is that I drag my heels and balk at the discipline of regular prayer. I need to remind myself that prayer isn't work. It works.*

ᴥ **Day 4** ᴥ

"Whenever I talk to God, I feel like I'm pleading and begging," a woman said to me. "What should I do?"

"If we can't beg God, who can we beg?" I said. "I'd just keep praying if I were you."

Inventory Focus: *Is prayer a regular part of your routine?*

☙ Day 5 ❧

Most religions have formal prayers and guidelines for praying. These include confession of wrongdoing, asking for forgiveness, expressing gratitude for help and gifts received, asking for guidance, asking for blessings on people we love or are trying to love, and praise.

Some people like to pray in the shower, others on their knees by their bed. Some like to pray in a group. People may bow their heads, or clasp their hands, or close their eyes. Some even consider thought a form of prayer.

We can talk out loud or silently think a prayer. We can even write letters in a God journal. Some people say long prayers in the morning. Others combine that with short little messages throughout the day to God.

How do you like to pray? What works for you?

Action: *Here's a recovery prayer based on* Alcoholics Anonymous, *the Big Book of Alcoholics Anonymous: "Thank you for keeping me straight yesterday. Please help me stay straight today. For the next twenty-four hours, I pray for knowledge of your will for me only and the power to carry that through. I pray that you might free my thinking of self-will, self-seeking, and wrong motives. I pray that in times of doubt and indecision, you might send your inspiration and guidance. I pray that you might send me the right thought, word, or action, and that you show me what my next step should be."*

You can pray for whatever you want, but asking to be shown God's Will and to be given the power to carry that through is usually a good bet.

❧ Day 6 ❧

My friend looked at all the devotees climbing a mountain on one of our trips to Tibet. They were peaceful, serene, radiant. My friend shook his head in awe. "Their whole life is a prayer," he said.

Gratitude Focus: *We can be grateful that even when we forget to pray, God doesn't forget us.*

❧ Day 7 ❧

Go ahead. Don't just think about praying. Talk to God.

Prayer: *Help me come close enough to you that even a little of you will rub off on me. Teach me the power of prayer.*

The Basics

✑ Day 1 ✑

"Isn't everyone codependent?" a woman asked me.

"Maybe," I said.

It is easy to get embroiled in other people's dramas. Isn't it even easier to see what other people need to do to take care of themselves, rather than tend to our own affairs? That's when we need to remember the basics of taking care of ourselves.

These basics include comfortable living arrangements, enough sleep, proper nutrition and hygiene, social contact, fun or pleasure, taking responsibility for our own emotions, earning enough money to pay our bills, taking responsibility for our own goals and dreams, and saying no—sometimes to others and sometimes to our own impulses.

My daughter introduced me to a computer game recently. It's a game where you create a city and get to rule the lives of the people in it. In this game, you get to decide where the people sleep, how much they sleep, when they eat, when they go to the bathroom, when they take a shower, whether they clean up after themselves, when they rest, whether they go to work so they can pay their bills and buy food, how much education they get, and how much they socialize. Kind of like playing God.

"You can make the people go crazy," my daughter explained. "All you have to do is not let them get enough sleep."

One of the meanings of "jaded" is being exhausted. Not getting enough sleep, not eating properly, not tending to our own emotions or our social needs can easily cause us to become jaded.

We can make ourselves feel crazy by not tending to the basics. It was tempting to torture the people in the game just to see how they reacted. Sometimes it's tempting to torture ourselves.

Value: Whether we call it self-care, taking responsibility for ourselves, being good to ourselves, or practicing the basics, that's the value we'll explore this week.

∾ Day 2 ∾

"I came from a crazy, neglectful family," a woman said. "I was fifty-two years old and I didn't know what it meant to take care of myself."

Application: The basics apply every day. It may be particularly important to focus on the basics when we first get into recovery from addiction or codependency. For recovering people, the basics expand to include attending recovery meetings and not taking the first drink, drug, or pill.

In times of high stress, grief, loss, or change, applying the most basic of the basics may be the only thing we can do to survive.

❧ Day 3 ❧

It's an interesting phenomenon. When I get so tired I can't think or work, I refuse to go to sleep, try to work harder, then wonder why I can't get anything done.

Challenge: *The basics may seem like such simple solutions that we overlook how important they really are.*

❧ Day 4 ❧

Alcoholics Anonymous uses the acronym HALT. It stands for not getting too hungry, angry, lonely, or tired. Do you need to remember to HALT?

Inventory Focus: *In Abraham Maslow's hierarchy of needs, people have basic needs. We won't be able to focus on the higher needs, such as spirituality and creativity, until the primary needs are met. How are you doing with taking care of your basic needs: sleep, nutrition, emotions, socialization? Are you taking the time for personal hygiene and keeping your home clean? Are you taking responsibility for your basic finances? Do you need medical care? Pay attention to how you feel when you tend to your basic needs. Pay attention to how you feel when you don't. Which feeling do you like better? Most of us have times when we are deprived of a good night's sleep or a meal, due to special circumstances. But if depriving ourselves of basic needs has become a way of life, maybe it's time to get back to basics and stop torturing ourselves.*

༄ **Day 5** ༄

"What are the rules for taking care of myself?" a woman asked me. I started to answer her by giving her a list, then I stopped myself. "The first rule is to learn to trust yourself."

Action: Make a list of your basics, then check in and see whether you're neglecting yourself in any area. When you're uncertain, ask yourself what you need to do to take care of yourself, or ask your Higher Power. Then listen and act on what you hear. Sometimes what we most need to do is so obvious and simple we can't see it. It may also be what we're resisting the most.

Remember, if you're going through deep grief or a time of intense change, you may need more sleep than usual.

༄ **Day 6** ༄

"My life changed when I stopped waiting for someone to rescue me and began taking responsibility for myself." I haven't heard this statement from just one person. I've heard it from thousands, including myself.

Gratitude Focus: We usually don't have the power to control what's going on around us, but we can be grateful that we always have the power to hunker down and take care of ourselves.

༄ **Day 7** ༄

Imagine wearing an energy meter with three zones: green for safe, yellow for caution, red for danger. You've got a strip that reads each area of your life: nutrition, sleep, hygiene, emotions, fun, social interaction, and, if you're in recovery, one for attending meetings.

As long as you stay in the green zone, you're safe. When you get into the yellow zone, it's time to pay careful attention. And once you get into the red zone, you could be in real danger. If your battery loses all its charge, you'll be stopped in your tracks.

Keep yourself charged. It actually gets fun, this taking-care-of-ourselves business, once you get the hang of it.

Prayer: *Thank you for promising to do for me what I cannot do for myself. Help me do my part. Help me remember to apply the basics, at least occasionally, with some tender loving care.*

Nurturing

༐ Day 1 ༐

A married couple I know were recently on vacation on an island in a foreign country. When the wife reached out to switch on the hotel lamp, she was surprised to be jolted by an electrical shock.

Then she got another shock. Her husband just glanced at her briefly, then said, "You'd better hurry up and get dressed or we'll be late for dinner. And be more careful with the lamps."

"I felt so hurt and angry," she said. "Not about getting shocked by the lamp. But by this man's total inability—or refusal—to be nurturing with me. His coldness was such a turnoff. But what I realized," she said, "is that's how I treat myself."

Some people don't appear to have a nurturing bone in their bodies. Other people seem to have been born as nurturers.

It took me awhile to understand that being nurturing is a value I can consciously choose to apply. It has taken me a long time and a lot of practice to get remotely comfortable with nurturing myself. I had good teachers: a sister who was nurturing and warm, an older woman who always made me feel safe and loved, a male friend who was kind and loving even during conflicts. The common denominator among the people I most enjoy is a high capacity to nurture. Sometimes it's okay to baby ourselves and others. What are you afraid of? Go ahead. Warm up. See how others turn to putty in your hands.

Value: Nurturing is a value that can be acquired. That's what we'll focus on this week.

✧ **Day 2** ✧

Some people tend to kick others when they're down. Sometimes that's how we treat ourselves. Confrontation, honesty, even tough love, can go a long way in cementing solid relationships. All these things go even further if they're delivered in a nurturing way.

Application: The best time to nurture is when people are down: blue, scared, sick, hurt, stressed, or depressed. Sometimes it's fun to be nurturing for no reason at all, other than it makes other people feel good. The nurturer also ends up feeling better.

✧ **Day 3** ✧

Being nurturing doesn't mean we need to be gushy, oversentimental, overprotective, smothering, obnoxious, insincere, or codependent. For a long time, that's what I thought it meant. It is possible to be a nurturing person and still maintain limits about how far we'll go.

Challenge: It can be difficult and even confusing to comprehend what it means to be nurturing if we haven't been nurtured ourselves. "Won't I lose my power?" we may think.

Some of the most powerful women and men I've known have the capacity to nurture others and themselves.

ᘓᕵ **Day 4** ᕵᘀ

Quick, a pop test. Which best describes you: warm or cold? Or are you warm on the inside and just appear cold to others?

Inventory Focus: *Were you nurtured as a child? Do a quick life review. Who are the people you've been involved with that you would describe as nurturing? Have your favorite people in your life been warm or cold? Have you had any experiences with being overnurturing? Do you need to learn to set boundaries when you nurture? Are you willing to warm up a little to others and yourself?*

ᘓᕵ **Day 5** ᕵᘀ

There's plenty of time for discipline, criticism, tough love, and advice—later. For now, just for a minute, let nurturing be enough. Nurturing gestures include nonsexual touch, a genuine smile, a sympathetic ear, gentle words that truly convey concern or encouragement.

Nurturing can come in the form of small efforts: a cup of tea with honey, a meal cooked with love, a shoulder massage.

Action: *Each day think of one small nurturing act you can do for someone else or for yourself. Maybe it's smiling at the guy behind the deli counter. Maybe it's telling someone what a good job they're doing. C'mon. Get creative. Make it sincere. You don't have to do anything you don't want to do. But you may need to push* yourself a little—use some oomph—to get started. Translate that warm heart into actions that convey love.

ᴄᴄ Day 6 ᴀᴠ

She ran a small stand, halfway up the mountain I was climbing in China. She didn't speak much English and I didn't speak Chinese. She didn't just slam a cup of coffee in front of me. She gently put it down and smiled. Then she pointed to the sunrise, helping me notice how beautiful it was. On my way down the mountain, late at night, when I arrived at her shop, she smiled and let me know how genuinely happy she was that I had made it back safe. Then she pulled out a chair and brought out a special treat—some kind of nut that I had never before tasted—and shared the delicacy with me.

She didn't ask. She just did those things. Tender loving care might not change our world. But it sure turns it into a nicer place.

Gratitude Focus: *We can be grateful for all the people who have touched our hearts and lives with love.*

ᴄᴄ Day 7 ᴀᴠ

See! You didn't have to be that scared of other people or yourself. Nurtured people are joyful people. Joyful people do their best.

Prayer: *Please give me a gentle touch with others and myself. Help me trust in love.*

The Dark Side

ᴖᴖ **Day 1** ᴖᴖ

Have you ever gone outside at night and looked closely at the new moon? Or looked through a telescope at the moon when it was crescent shaped? Although what we see is a bright slice, we know there's more. Even when the moon is full and lights the night sky, there's a dark side to the moon.

There's a dark side to us too. We all experience jealousy, envy, bitterness, resentment. How about neediness? Ugh. Who wants to shine a light on that?

What about all those fears? Fear of failure, fear of success, fear of intimacy, fear of going broke, fear of staying broke, fear of abandonment, fear that we're essentially unlovable, fear of the unknown, fear of growing old, fear of being alone, fear of being with someone, fear of losing control.

Then there are other parts of us that we would prefer to keep darkened and out of sight, parts such as greed, dishonesty, intolerance, disgust, hatred. Although some people have no problem showing anger, others of us prefer to keep that out of sight too. And what about our manipulative part? Who wants anyone to see that?

Some of us may even consider the dark side of ourselves forbidden. We may refuse to acknowledge it exists because we believe it's *wrong.* Not acknowledging our dark side doesn't wish it out of existence, any more than not seeing the dark side of the moon makes it disappear.

Most sane people agree that they don't want to be controlled by their dark side. We don't want parts of ourselves—jealousy, neediness, greed—to control our behaviors. But when we don't acknowledge these emotions and traits, they can gain control. The more we try to repress something, the more it fights for its life.

Stand back. Don't be afraid. Shine a light on that dark part. At least look at it briefly. Acknowledge it's there. Take some of the pressure off. Let yourself be well rounded, instead of one dimensional.

Take it a step further. Share those darker parts with others, so they can shine a light on those parts of themselves. Experience how much easier it is not to act needy, not to speak bitterly, and not to look disgusted when you acknowledge those feelings.

Value: We don't just have a light side, a bright side. Nobody is always loving, always kind, always generous, always thoughtful. Honestly acknowledging our character defects is the value this week.

✨ Day 2 ✨

While we don't want to act on our dark side, most of us do from time to time. Acknowledging that it's there helps give us the power to neutralize it, change, and join the human race.

Application: When we find ourselves fighting who we are or feeling guilty for how we really feel, it may be time to look at our dark side. When we feel like we need to be more in control of what we feel and find in ourselves, a good dose of accepting who we really are may be just the value we need to apply.

೮ಾ **Day 3** ᵔ

It's easy to believe that loving ourselves unconditionally means only accepting our lighter, brighter parts. Most of us have a lot of guilt about who we really are.

Challenge: The hardest part about seeing the dark side of ourselves is getting in touch with what we may see as forbidden and unacceptable.

೮ಾ **Day 4** ᵔ

What are the emotions you've forbidden yourself to feel?

Inventory Focus: Are there parts of yourself that you're repressing, instead of expressing? Each week, you've been working on an inventory focus related to the value of the week. In Twelve Step programs, people are encouraged to do regular inventories of their shortcomings, their dark side. After a huge sweep of an inventory, they're encouraged to make daily checks to monitor their shortcomings. Then they're encouraged to discuss this part of themselves with God and with another human being. Most religions have some sort of formalized ritual for expressing and shining light on the dark side that all human beings have. How do you deal with your dark side? Have you looked at it lately? Are you at least somewhat willing to look at and accept the dark part of yourself and others?

✌ **Day 5** ✌

Honesty is the best policy.

Action: You are not your behaviors. You are not your emotions. Your behaviors are what you do; your emotions are what you feel. Each day, pause for a moment. Ask yourself what you're really feeling. If you're not sure, listen to the tone of your voice and your thoughts. Those are good clues. Many people find it helpful to write about what they're feeling in a journal or diary. Make sure no one has access to your journal, then have at it. Write it all out. Or tell another person what you're feeling, thinking, having a hard time with. Sometimes sharing what we're going through with one other person takes the pressure off.

If you're in a Twelve Step program, do the Fourth and Fifth Steps. If you're having a lot of guilt or an unusually hard time with some aspects of yourself, you might want either to get professional help or to talk to a clergyperson. Tell your Higher Power who you really are. Sometimes honest awareness, acknowledgment, and acceptance are all that's required. There may be parts of yourself that you want to change, but honest acceptance is how change begins.

✌ **Day 6** ✌

A friend called me on the phone and burst into a tirade of envy, resentment, anger, bitterness. I listened.

"I'm not sure what to do," I said, when he finished.

"You don't have to do anything," he said. "Just listen."

Gratitude Focus: We can be grateful for people who have

the courage to share their dark side with us. We can be grateful for the people with whom we feel safe enough to talk honestly. We can also be grateful for all parts of ourselves and others. Gratitude doesn't imply approval. In this case, it can be a tool to promote unconditional acceptance and love.

⟡ Day 7 ⟡

"I hate being this vulnerable," I said to a friend after sharing some of what I thought were particularly unacceptable emotions and feelings with him. I had just spent fifteen minutes displaying an entire side of myself that I would have preferred didn't exist.

"I love your power and your strength, Melody," he said. "But I think you're even more beautiful when you're human and vulnerable."

Hmmm. Maybe the dark side of that moon is more beautiful than we thought.

Prayer: *Give me the courage to be honest about myself. Keep me from causing harm to myself or others. Help me learn about the tremendous power and healing of honestly sharing who I really am.*

An Open Mind

ꕔꕐ **Day 1** ꕔꕐ

"It was the night of my weekly recovery group," a woman said to me. "I had to make myself attend the meeting. We had a guest speaker from out of town, and everyone had been buzzing about this speaker for weeks.

"'Oh, Corky's coming. Have you heard about Corky? Don't miss the meeting; Corky will be there to talk that night. He's the best.' I was so sick of hearing about Corky. I didn't know who he was, and I didn't care. I just couldn't stomach all this gushing. By the time I got to the meeting, the only chair open was right next to Corky. I was so turned off and disgusted. I just couldn't stand all this naive raving.

"I sat through the meeting. Barely heard a word this guy said. At the end of the meeting, when it came time to hold hands and say the prayer, I couldn't stand the thought of putting my hand in his. But I did.

"When I got home from attending the group that evening, my husband asked me how it went. So I told him the whole story, about Corky, about everyone being so excited this guy was coming to town, about my decision not to be involved with this idolization of some stupid guy named Corky.

" 'Don't you know who that is?' my husband said. I told him the only thing I knew was that he went by the nickname Corky. My husband pointed to the stack of books at my bedside—all written by the same author. My favorite author in the entire world.

" 'It's him,' my husband said. 'It's the guy you read every night. Corky is just his nickname.' I felt this wave of horror go through me. I had wanted to meet this guy for years. I loved his mind. I loved his work. And here I had sat right next to him—even held his hand—and I hadn't even heard a word he said or appreciated the opportunity I had to meet him.

"I've seen him around a few times since that night," my friend added. "I haven't had the courage to tell him my story yet. Maybe someday I will. Until then, I'm working hard to remember the lesson of that night: keep an open mind or you might miss something or someone really valuable in your life."

Closing our mind and our heart can cause us to lose a lot more than a chance to meet someone we revere. We can miss the true beauty and wisdom in people who at first glance look ordinary. We can miss opportunities and ideas that could change our lives. We can overlook danger signs. And sometimes, we can embarrass ourselves.

Value: We can call it dropping our assumptions or judgments, staying aware, or keeping an open mind. Whatever words we use to describe this state, that's the value this week.

ꙮ Day 2 ꙮ

Whenever we start thinking we've seen, heard, or done it

all, we can be assured we haven't. Something new is just around the corner.

Application: Whenever lazy thinking kicks in, whenever we find ourselves spouting judgments about something before we've checked it out, whenever we start relying on assumptions and not paying attention to what we see, hear, and feel, it may be time to open our mind.

ᘓᖇ Day 3 ᖇᘐ

There are so many rip-off artists and scams in the world. There's so much that disappoints us. We get excited about someone or something, then we check it out and find it's not what everyone says it is. Sometimes negative thinking is easier and more realistic.

Sometimes I get so busy that I do what I call *lazy thinking.* I ignore little warning signs, things that make my gut go *click.* Or I rely on my assumptions because it takes less work, rather than checking things out for myself.

Yes, sometimes we're disappointed. Sometimes the price to pay for staying aware is we discover something that hurts our feelings or disappoints us. But every once in a while, something or someone comes along that's a pleasant and rewarding surprise.

Challenge: The hardest thing about staying open is that it requires constant, diligent effort and work.

ᘓᖇ Day 4 ᖇᘐ

I was on a train in China with my hiking partner. The train's departure time was delayed. We sat across a table from a man and woman who looked to be in their late twenties or early thirties. The delay in departing went on and on. Like us, the couple we sat across from had brought a large bag of snack foods onto the train.

"They remind me of us," I said in a voice they could clearly hear. I didn't think this couple spoke English. "Kind of cute, but nerdy. And look," I said. "They've already eaten all their snacks, and we haven't even left the station."

Finally, the train took off. About half an hour into the ride, the man across from us smiled. "So, where are you guys from?" he asked in perfect English.

We can prejudge people to be gods and saints, then become disappointed when we find out they're not. We can assume that others have nothing to teach us because of their humble or simple lifestyles. Some people say that to *assume* makes an *ass* out of *u* and *me*. Usually when I assume, it simply irritates other people and makes an ass out of me.

> **Inventory Focus:** *Are you prejudging a situation or a person right now? Do you have a history of pre-deciding how something or someone is going to be, then plowing ahead based on that decision instead of staying aware and open? Is life trying to get your attention right now? Sometimes circumstances change. There's no substitute for daily awareness.*

Day 5

See for yourself.

> **Action:** *Before you get out of bed in the morning, try to put all ideas you have about that day out of your mind. Then make a deliberate decision to stay open to all the*

possibilities. Cultivate an attitude of curiosity. If you are running into a series of events where assumptions have gotten you into trouble, you may want to slow down and put extra effort into checking things out. Remember that, when in doubt, it's okay to ask.

⟡ **Day 6** ⟡

If life had only happened the way I thought it would, I'd still be a drug-using junkie or dead.

Gratitude Focus: *Thank God there's so much more to life than we think there is.*

⟡ **Day 7** ⟡

Life hasn't lost its wonder and awe. We have. If we just open our mind a little, we'll see how magical the world can be.

Prayer: *Help me to stay open and aware. Help me to see everything you want me to see.*

Crazy People Make Us Crazy

ᘜᖇ Day 1 ᖇᘜ

"He's making me crazy. I don't understand. Why would someone say they were going to do one thing, then do something so different from what they say? He looks so good and talks so good. His promises sound so, so real, but then everything falls apart. I end up doing all this work, and he just disappears. I get so dang angry. Then about the time I'm ready to blow a gasket, he calls, charms my socks off, and the whole cycle starts over again. I walk away, scratching my head and wondering, 'What's wrong with me? Did I just imagine this whole thing? Did I overreact?' I don't get it. I don't understand."

Maybe it's time for an Al-Anon meeting.

"And when we're talking on the phone, I feel like I'm the only one for him. But then when I see him, I know he's lying to me. I know he's seeing someone else and standing there looking me right in the eyes and lying about it. When I ask him, he says, 'Your insecurity is enchanting, and you're usually such a together person.' I don't understand why I feel so insane."

Maybe it's time for an Al-Anon meeting.

"And then I catch him straight-out lying to me, and I blow up. I just can't stand that lying stuff, especially when

I knew all the time he was lying to me and he denied it. I put up with it and put up with it and then finally I can't take it anymore. By the time I blow up, he's standing there looking calm and serene and I'm acting like an insane person."

Crazy people make us feel crazy. It's not you. It's him. How about that meeting?

"And then he calls a few days later, and he says how sorry he is and I can tell he's sorry. Before I know it, I've forgotten about everything that happened, and it starts all over again. I keep wondering whether I'm being used, and then I look at him and I just feel so guilty for everything I'm feeling and thinking. Oh yeah. That Al-Anon meeting."

Step One: Powerless over people, places, and things. My life has become unmanageable. Take a deep breath. Say it again. Then say it one more time. Crazy people make us feel crazy. It will happen every time.

Value: Detach in love. Disentangle. Un-embroil *yourself from other people's insanity so you can be restored to sanity. It's a value many of us learned the hard way, and it's the one we'll focus on this week.*

∽ Day 2 ∾

Other people's dramas are so seductive. The more we love someone, the easier it is to become embroiled. You may think, "I can't let go." Yes, you can. If you can't detach in love, just detach. Let love come later.

Application: Whenever we can't stop talking or thinking about someone else, it's time to detach. If we feel like someone else is making us crazy and we can't figure out how to help them, it's time to help ourselves.

ᘓᕦ **Day 3** ᕤᘏ

"My husband is using cocaine," a woman said. "He won't listen to me when I tell him to stop. So, how about this? I'll pop the movie *Blow*, about cocaine abuse, into the VCR and just keep playing it over and over until he gets the message."

"How about this," I said. "You go to an Al-Anon meeting and get some help for yourself."

The first time we're exposed to the value of detaching, it can seem so improbable and unlikely. After a while, we begin to see how well detaching works. When we let go of what we cannot change, the other person begins to experience his or her own consequences. The other person may or may not do what we want them to do, but because we've been restored to sanity, a clear path opens for us. The things we do actually begin to help.

The first time we practice detachment is the hardest. Later, it becomes easier.

Challenge: *No matter how long we have practiced the value of detachment, recognizing when we need to do it can still be the hardest part.*

ᘓᕦ **Day 4** ᕤᘏ

Anger, fear, sadness, betrayal—a lot of emotions can run through us when we stop trying to change the other person and start focusing on taking care of ourselves. The good news is that we're finally feeling our own feelings instead of trying to figure out what the other person feels.

Maybe all those feelings we've been avoiding aren't the opposite of love. Those feelings could be an important step on the path to love.

Inventory Focus: Is there a relationship in your life right now that's bugging you? Are you willing to explore detachment as a means to improving the relationship and regaining your peace?

☜ Day 5 ☞

"I'm making myself nuts today," I said to a friend. "I'm going to stop what I'm doing and go to bed."

Sometimes the crazy person I need to detach from is me.

Action: You may find great relief by practicing Step One of Al-Anon. You admit that you are powerless over alcohol (or people, places, and things) and that your life has become unmanageable. You focus on this Step, instead of on your obsession. It is also helpful to talk to someone else who understands and practices detachment. You may have to repeatedly focus on this value, sometimes many times a day, when someone else's insanity is spilling into your life.

☜ Day 6 ☞

"When my son was using drugs and I finally had to let go, it was one of the hardest experiences in my life," a woman said. "Now, years later, looking back at the experience, I see that he was my teacher for detaching in love."

Gratitude Focus: We can be grateful for all the people, places, and things that teach us—the hard way—about the value of detaching in love. We can also be grateful for all the people who give us positive support for doing that.

✐ **Day 7** ✐

Crazy people make us crazy if we let them.

> **Prayer:** *Please teach me to love and live without hanging on so tightly. Give me the courage to walk my own path and trust you to guide others on their paths.*

Laughter

ᥰ Day 1 ᥴ

I walked out the bakery door holding my crescent and coffee. I looked down. On the sidewalk lay a large dog. He was on his back, motionless. A crowd of people was gathering around and staring.

"Oh my God," I said.

A man walked up to me. "What's the matter?" he asked. "Haven't you ever seen a dead dog before?"

I was horrified. Then I saw the glimmer of a smile on the man's face. I looked more closely. This is Los Angeles. Even dogs want to be actors. The owner had told the dog to play dead instead of sit while he was in the bakery. I chuckled and then walked to my car.

I first learned about the value of laughter the year after I got out of treatment for my chemical dependency. I had a job working for a law firm in a small town. I was so frightened—of life, of myself, of whether I could stay sober. I didn't talk much those days. I was all bound up inside of myself.

I spent a lot of time working alongside a pretty woman in her late twenties, a paralegal in the firm. Often our tasks consisted of rather repetitive, unexciting chores. Mailing, filing, organizing massive stacks of correspondence and legal documents for real estate transactions, and typing wills. This was in the old days, before electric typewriters, before computers. Wills had to be typed perfectly; we couldn't use correction fluid or erasers. It wasn't uncommon to get to the last line of the page and make a mistake.

There was nothing particularly exciting happening in my world as I struggled to learn the early disciplines of staying sober and being responsible. What I remember most was working alongside this woman, and her ability to laugh at herself, at her tasks, at the sometimes gruesome and boring nature of life. I hadn't been around anyone with a sense of humor. To this day, I don't think she knows how much she affected me and how much she taught me. I can't even remember her name, but I remember the lesson. She taught me to laugh.

Laughter takes the pressure off and lightens the load. We can actually feel our body and our chemistry change when the corners of the mouth turn upward toward the heavens in a smile.

Value: Whether it's a slight chuckle from deadpan humor or a laugh that makes your belly ache and tears stream down your face, laughter is the value for this week.

୧୨ Day 2 ୧୨

I went to see a therapist a few months after my son's death. He listened to my story and carefully explained how the grieving process would take time, and how I wasn't going to feel happy or even comfortable for a while.

He explained there wasn't a lot I could *do* to change my situation, speed things up, or dull the pain.

"But there's one thing that's crucial," he said. "And you must start doing it right away."

"What's that?" I asked.

"Remember the law of humor," he said. "Remember to let yourself laugh."

We don't want to make fun of other people's circumstances. We don't want to mask pain with false laughter. But no matter what circumstance we're going through, laughter isn't just optional. It's essential. Humor is a law.

Application: Whenever we can't remember the last time we laughed, it's time to do it.

❧ Day 3 ❧

Go ahead. Have a good laugh.

Challenge: See? Nothing about laughing is hard.

❧ Day 4 ❧

Is laughter a regular part of your emotional diet?

Inventory Focus: Are you going through such a tough, intense, or challenging situation right now that you're forgetting to laugh? Are you telling yourself your situation is so glum that it would be disrespectful to indulge in laughter? Maybe it's exactly what you and the people around you need. There are times when it's inappropriate and disrespectful to laugh, but don't let those times go on too long. We can develop a sense of humor and a sense of timing.

༼ Day 5 ༽

What makes you laugh? I love slapstick humor and really dumb stuff, like the Ernest movies, when he kept getting marker all over his face while on jury duty. The harder he would try to stop doing it, the more marker he would get on himself.

People who have a sense of humor about their flaws and mistakes make me laugh. "I know there's a value in every relationship we've been in. And I can see the value in most of mine—even the worst," a friend explained. "But that particular one, hard as I try, I just can't find the value, unless it's 'Don't be with someone who repulses you.'"

What tickles you?

Action: Who in your life makes you laugh? Enjoy them. What movies and TV shows make you laugh? Watch them. What books, radio shows, or jokes lighten you? Don't go to sleep at night until you've had at least one good laugh each day. If you can't find anything funny right now in your life, let yourself remember a time or experience that was funny.

༼ Day 6 ༽

People who make us laugh are bright spots in our lives.

Gratitude Focus: We can be grateful for the people who help us laugh.

༼ Day 7 ༽

Sometimes people don't get our one-liners. Sometimes they do and just frown with a disapproving look that makes us cringe. Sometimes we laugh at the wrong time or wrong place. But please don't stop laughing. We need all the help we can get to remember to laugh and to smile.

Sometimes, when I go to sleep at night, I swear I hear cherubs giggling.

Prayer: *Please grant me a sense of humor. Send me something or someone special to make me smile.*

Love-ability

෴ Day 1 ෴

A friend of mine recently told me how he met his wife. He had watched her walk by his store every day for a year, with her young son. She also happened to be a friend of his neighbor.

"Fix me up," he suggested to his neighbor. "We'll go on a double date. I really want to meet her." Unfortunately, the neighbor never got around to setting up that first date.

Finally my friend devised a plan. Every day when she walked by the store, they said hello to each other, but she never stopped to chat. This day, he was ready. He had his store keys in hand. "Would it be all right if I walked with you for a while?" he asked when she walked by.

"Don't you have to mind your store?"

"I'll lock it up," he said.

"You don't have to do that," she said. "We can sit here and chat."

That Friday, they had their first date. She was nervous.

The next weekend, they went out again. She was still nervous. He turned to her. "You can relax," he said. "I'm not going to try anything inappropriate. I just want to enjoy your company." As time passed, she did relax, and they continued to become friends. Three years later, they were married in a small ceremony. "I didn't want to overwhelm her son," my friend recalled.

He wrote his wedding vows. He promised to love her and care for her all of his life. He promised to love her son and protect him, as if he were his own. She lit up his life, he said, and he was grateful for her promise of companionship for the rest of their lives.

My friend is a lucky man, but not just because he found someone he truly loves. He is lucky because he is able to recognize the gift of his wife's love. Most of us have the ability to see when we have been harmed, hurt, or slighted, when we're not loved or treated the way we'd like to be. But we can learn to see those acts—big and small— when someone shows us love. They are the greatest gifts of all.

Value: Call it believing we deserve love, lovability, or love-ability, the value for this week is opening our eyes and hearts so we can see and receive love from others— friends, family, romantic involvements, and God.

⌘ Day 2 ⌘

I was in Bali helping a friend host a convention. He took me to his house. I visited with his wife and met his new baby. Before I left, he gave me a tour of his home. As I looked around his home I glanced at myself in a mirror. I felt a shock of horror, started to walk away, then spun back for another look.

"I can't believe I look like that," I said in utter disgust.

My friend paused, looked in the mirror, and said, "You can't believe how much time I spend staring in that thing, wishing I looked different too."

Take a look in the mirror. If you don't like what you see, take another look. This time try seeing with the eyes of love.

Application: *Whenever we look in the mirror and wonder how anyone could possibly ever love us or when that might happen, it's time to work on our love-ability.*

ᦱ Day 3 ᦱ

I know. We didn't get loved the way we wanted. Some of us have spent years picking through the messy issues of parents who had unusual ways of showing love or who didn't show love at all.

We may have had spouses who were dreadful at showing love. Issues like alcoholism and other dysfunctions can genuinely interfere with a person's ability to love. Some of us took that personally. We looked around and the only conclusion we could come up with is that we weren't lovable.

Some of us need to grieve the absence of love in our family of origin. We may have missed an important emotional lesson while growing up, and we barely realize it. That lesson is understanding how lovable we are.

Some of us learned to protect ourselves by caring for others, while refusing to let love into our own lives. We found that it is easier to shut down and not be open to love, rather than be denied love.

After a while, we stop seeing the love that is there for us. We refuse the small gestures that may mean a tremendous amount to the person offering them. These gestures include words of concern, support, understanding, assistance, kindness, or a genuine expression of like or love. If we don't believe we're lovable, if we're not open to seeing and receiving love, we're going to miss more than just the love we missed in our childhood. We're going to miss the love that is available for us now.

Challenge: *The hardest part about letting people give us love can be softening that tough shell enough to let the gentle words and acts of love sink in.*

ಲ Day 4 ೲ

"I met with an old boyfriend two years after I broke up with him. I was astounded by how much he loved me. I had broken up with him because I was irritated that he wasn't loving me the way I wanted to be loved. I had some romantic ideas about how love should look and feel. Maybe the problem wasn't him not loving me. Maybe the problem was me not believing I deserved to be loved."

We can get so caught up in our expectations of how love should be shown that we don't see the reality of how people actually show love for us.

Inventory Focus: *Are you missing love in your life right now? Are you missing it because it's not there, because you're not seeing it, or because you're chasing it away? When is the last time you accepted an offer of help from a friend? How do you respond when someone you care about touches your arm? When someone says he or she loves you, whether it's a friend or romantic interest, how do you feel? Do you do all the giving just so you can stay in control? Set boundaries, but don't throw the baby out with the bathwater.*

❧ **Day 5** ❧

Could you soften up just a little bit and let someone love you? Can you at least start by believing someone cares?

Action: The next time someone offers to do something nice for you, don't instantly reject the offer. If it feels appropriate, accept the offer. (Maybe push yourself a little here.) Don't accept another's kindness to make that person feel good. Do it for you.

❧ **Day 6** ❧

One of people's universal fears is the fear of rejection. It doesn't make sense to keep rejecting ourselves.

Gratitude Focus: Heads up. Be aware. We can be grateful each time someone—or God—shows kindness or love to us.

❧ **Day 7** ❧

Come down to earth. Accept the little gestures of kindness and love. It's the gateway to heaven.

Prayer: Higher Power, please help me stop sabotaging love. Show me that it's the greatest gift of all.

Blessings

ᆇ **Day 1** ᆇ

I was out with a married couple for dinner, when the husband sneezed.

"God bless you," I said.

He sneezed again. "Bless you," I said.

Then he sneezed again and again.

"He sneezes all the time," his wife said. "I think he does it on purpose. He just wants people to bless him."

"Who doesn't want that?" I said.

My first experience with the value of blessing people happened in the early years of my sobriety. I wanted a job that someone else was given. I felt envious and resentful. Twelve Step programs and religions teach us a basic formula to cure ill will: pray for those you resent. Pray for God to shower blessings and happiness on those people. Pray for these blessings each time the resentment—or any hint of ill will—enters your mind.

So I did. I prayed twenty or more times a day because that is how often I resented this person. I didn't feel like praying for blessings. I decided to pray because the envy and bitter feelings were consuming me.

Over a period of months, I watched the situation transform. This person became my friend and mentor.

I eventually got a new position that I really wanted. I learned two things. Other people don't have anything that belongs to me. And praying for blessings on people is a double whammy. They get blessed, and so do we.

Blessings are not just a tool to cure ill will and resentment—although that would be plenty. Blessings, like gentle rain or sunshine, are in this world for all. Don't wait for people to sneeze to bless them. Be an active participant in spreading goodwill.

Value: Blessing our enemies, our loved ones, and ourselves is the value for this week.

༄ Day 2 ༅

Many people agree that thoughts are a form of prayer.

Application: Whenever we find ourselves thinking negative thoughts about someone in our lives, it's time to change our intentions toward that person. It's time to pray for only good things for that person.

༄ Day 3 ༅

It can be tough to stop resenting someone. It takes a deliberate decision—an oomph—to turn our thinking around. For starters, it can be helpful to remember that those around us eventually grow weary of listening to us whine, even if we were wronged. There is a point where enough is enough.

We need to feel our emotions. We don't want to get into repression or denial, but once we've felt the emotion, it's time to let it go and turn the situation around. Envy and ill will can be a constant undercurrent in our thinking, if we don't consciously seek to pluck out these emotions. It may feel like other people are constantly getting the good luck, that we have none, and that the good luck others are getting was somehow taken from us. It's not true. And resenting others and spreading ill will doesn't help us or improve our situation.

"There's a lot of haters out there in the world," a man said to me. "They don't even know they're spreading hate by the envious, bitter little thoughts they think."

Challenge: *The hardest part about spreading blessings around can be remembering to ask God to bless us.*

ꙮ Day 4 ꙮ

"What were you looking for on that quest?" someone asked me about the two trips I had taken to China and Tibet to climb and visit five holy mountains.

"I'm never quite sure what I'm looking for until I find it," I said. "But I became acutely aware on that trip what I had lost, and what I missed."

The 1990s had been hard on me. That period of time was not the dark *night* of the soul; it was the dark *decade* of the soul. I became acutely aware in China that what I missed and yearned for was the feeling of being blessed by God.

Inventory Focus: *Do you feel blessed? Would you like to feel blessed? Are you willing to forgo resenting your enemies and begin blessing them instead?*

ꙮ Day 5 ꙮ

Action: *Ask God to bless your enemies, people you're*

envious of, people you're angry with, people you're concerned about, people you love. Use their names when you say the blessing. Ask God to bless each person's health, finances, all areas of his or her life. Ask God to pour down blessings on that person. Say it until you mean it, until you feel the blessing in your heart. If you're praying for someone you resent, say the blessing each time that person's name pops into your mind. Whenever a friend or a loved one comes to mind, say a special blessing for that person too. In your prayer time, take a moment to ask God to bless you. Whenever you start a project, your day at work, a meeting, or even a night of fun with friends, you can say a silent little prayer asking God to bless that too. Ask God to bless the people you're giving to and serving. While you're at it, ask God to bless our country and the world.

ᘯᕽ Day 6 ᕽᘯ

I walked into the Sanctuario de Chimayo, a small chapel in Chimayo, New Mexico, known throughout the world for its healing powers. When I walked through the front door, a priest approached me and gently put his hand on my forehead.

"Blessings," he said. "God bless you, child."

I started crying, the blessing felt that good in my heart.

It can be a spiritual treat—a nice surprise and a reward —to get a blessing from a clergyperson. But remember, we've all been vested with the power to bless.

Gratitude Focus: We can be grateful for every chance we get to bless others. We can be assured that those blessings will rain down equally on others and on us. While we're at it, we can look around and be grateful for the blessings we already have.

❧ Day 7 ☙

Just ask for blessings. Extend blessings toward others. Then leave the details of the blessings—the how, when, and where—to God. It won't take long before we see how well blessings work. Blessings are one way we can participate in the love and good in the world.

Prayer: *Bless me and help me remember to bless others every day.*

One Day at a Time

෴ Day 1 ෴

My best friend was going through some tough situations in her life. I was in the midst of a hard stretch too. We didn't particularly like the things we had to do in our lives. We talked about our feelings and decided that what we were going through was necessary and important, even though we didn't like it. We expressed gratitude for our lives.

"It's still a dreadful time," I said.

"Brutal," she said. "I guess we're back to the old one-day-at-a-time approach. We're so lucky. What do people do that haven't learned that gem?"

There are times when we can look at the stretch ahead and like what we see. Taking life one day at a time is still a good idea, even when things are going well.

Taking life one day at a time can be particularly useful when the road ahead looks dreadful. We may not even know where to start with some challenges. That's when taking life one day at a time is essential.

"I've been using alcohol and other drugs every day since I've been twelve years old," I said to my counselor years ago in treatment. "Now you're telling me I need to stay sober the rest of my life. Plus get a job. And a life. How am I going to do that?"

"One day at a time," she said. She was right. Sometimes I had to take life one minute at a time or one hour at a time. And all these years later, it still works.

Value: Taking life one day at a time is the gem we'll focus on this week.

✎ Day 2 ✎

"One day at a time" isn't a value I acquired because I wanted to. I had to. Now I apply it because I want to.

Application: Sailing through life? Falling in love? Plenty of money? Or maybe things aren't going that well. Lonely? Dealing with relationship issues? Not sure how the relationship will work out? Your boss is driving you nuts, but you don't want to quit? Concerned about your child? Whatever circumstances we find ourselves in, taking each day as it comes is a good idea.

✎ Day 3 ✎

"Are you always this happy?" I asked my favorite clerk at the grocery store.

"I am today," he said.

Doing anything forever—even being happy—can seem like too much. The good news is that we don't have to do anything forever. Just today.

Challenge: The hardest part about taking life one day at a time is remembering that the present moment is all we have.

∽ Day 4 ∾

It's easy to look at all the tasks and unsolved problems and feel so pressured that we get paralyzed and don't get anything done. It takes discipline to gather in our scattered forces and focus on one thing, one day, one step, and sometimes one hour—even when taking only that one step can seem so trivial in the face of all that looms.

Would you rather try to do everything at once and get nothing done, or take one small step and do that well? Remember, one plus one equals two.

Inventory Focus: Are you creating unnecessary fear and drama by taking on more than you can handle? Are you willing to trade in the I'm-out-of-control-and-overwhelmed feeling for a sense of manageability? Do you have any history with deliberately living life one day or one step at a time? How did that work? Plans, goals, and dreams are good, but the only way to get there is one day at a time.

∽ Day 5 ∾

Let go of the fear. Feel it, then breathe it out. Let go of the frustration, the overwhelmed feelings, the panic. Quiet yourself. Then pick one task, one simple thing to do. Then focus on only that. Or go to your calendar and circle today. Today is the only day you've got, and today is enough.

Action: If you're working on a project, break it down into components, and work on one small part. Don't think about the rest. If what's overwhelming you is a flurry of tasks and problems, make a list, then pick one thing and focus on doing that. Then cross it off your list and do another. If you're going through a tough stretch in your life, don't think about all the days that loom ahead. Make whatever appointments and plans you need to make, then focus only on today. If you're experiencing something tough, like a divorce or early sobriety, you may want to break your days into smaller parts, such as hours, mornings, afternoons, and evenings. Don't think about facing anything more than that chunk of time. Then when you get to the next chunk, focus on that. If the beast of anxiety starts roaring, quiet it by deliberately turning your attention to small steps.

ᴏ᷉ᴗ Day 6 ᴗ᷉ᴏ

Thank God for the ability to break life down into days.

Gratitude Focus: *We can start and end each day by being grateful for everything that happened in it and the help we encountered along the way.*

ᴏ᷉ᴗ Day 7 ᴗ᷉ᴏ

We can climb the highest mountains and navigate the darkest valleys. We can do anything. Just not all at once.

Prayer: *Teach me how to go anywhere—at least wherever you want me to go—by taking it one day and one step at a time. Show me how much beauty and joy there are when I live life that way.*

Easy Does It

७२० Day 1 ᏗᏅᏉ

So, you surrendered. You let go. Now you're ready to face a particular challenge. So you hunker down and garner all your forces. And you hit the wall again.

"What's wrong?" you may ask. "I'm doing all the spiritual things I'm supposed to do. And things still aren't working. I can't get anywhere."

Did you ever try to get a key to unlock a door, and you tried and tried, and the key just wouldn't open it? The harder you tried, the more frustrated you became. So you stopped trying for a while, relaxed, and tried again. Voilà. The key fit perfectly and the slightest turn unlocked the door.

Many of us live our lives that way. While some people may not try at all, we may be trying too hard. There's a gentler way of being in the world, of trying things, doing things, going about our business.

Whether I'm tackling a specific project, enjoying a new relationship, or grinding through some miserable situation, my first inclination is to force myself and try too hard. If one cup of tea tastes good, I'll drink five. If I want to express love or concern for someone, I'll overdo it.

"If it's worth doing, it's worth doing well," doesn't

mean if it's worth doing, try harder and harder. Doing it well means relaxing and letting the actions unfold— gently, naturally, without force. We don't have to make things happen. We can learn to take our part in letting them happen. It is really okay to ease up a little. We don't have to think that hard, try that hard, feel that hard, *do* quite so much. Pull back a little. Relax.

When force and trying harder doesn't do it, try something else.

Value: "Easy does it" is the value this week.

✎ Day 2 ✎

It's an old saying from Alcoholics Anonymous, and you may have seen it on the bumper sticker of a car: "Easy does it." It's also an ancient Buddhist value. And it's one of the points found in Winnie-the-Pooh stories. There's a natural order, rhythm, and movement to the flow of life. We can't tap into it when we're trying too hard. The trick is relaxing and allowing that flow to find and include us.

Application: Whenever we're trying harder and accomplishing less, it may be time to ease up.

✎ Day 3 ✎

"Why does doing this have to be so hard?" I asked a friend one day.

"It doesn't," he said.

Challenge: Unquestionably, life can be tough and challenging at times. It hurts. It can be scary and confusing. Many of us have had to garner great amounts of strength and courage to face difficult situations. There are times when endurance and rising to the occasion are important survival skills. It's equally important to know when an easy-does-it approach is enough.

◡ **Day 4** ◠

Are you scared that if you don't try harder it won't get done? Do you struggle with the extremes of not trying at all and trying too hard?

Inventory Focus: *Are you trying to force something to happen? Is that working out well for you? Instead of believing that you have to make it happen all by yourself, by the sheer exertion of strength and will, try to relax and gently ease into it. Try to trust that things will work out well, that you're not alone, and that you're part of a greater plan. Are you willing to try that, instead of trying harder? Sometimes when things don't work out, it's because you're trying to do the wrong thing. Other times, it's because you're doing the right thing, but trying too hard. You won't know which approach is best until you step back.*

◡ **Day 5** ◠

Don't make it happen. Let it unfold.

Action: *Stop. Restrain yourself. Relax. Now try again —gently. Stop as often as you need to, whether it's in a conversation, going through your day, or working on a project. There are times when less really is more.*

ᴄᴠᴀ **Day 6** ᴀᴠᴄ

I watched a friend set up beach chairs and an umbrella. He was grunting, groaning, trying with all his might to accomplish a simple task. After he finished, he looked around and clapped the sand off his hands.

"I'm pretty dumb," he said. "It didn't have to be that hard or that much work."

Yes, life really can be easier. Relaxing and letting it unfold can seem too simple and easy at times. What if we really knew that it was okay to gently go about our lives, living and working and handling things at a relaxed pace? What if we knew it was okay to gently take care of ourselves, and that a force would be present to guide us and help us accomplish each task, each problem, in fact, all the parts of our lives?

Life experience truly has taught me that when I relax, I am so much more capable of experiencing great happiness as well as simple joys. Things get done, problems get solved, and my needs get met.

Gratitude Focus: *We can be grateful for all the situations that teach and remind us that "easy does it" works.*

ᴄᴠᴀ **Day 7** ᴀᴠᴄ

If we've prayed for knowledge of God's Will for us and the power to carry that out, then relax. Trust that power. We don't have to do it by force or on our own.

Prayer: *Help me let go of my fears and anxieties. Teach me that relaxing—an easy-does-it approach—is the way to serenity.*

Patience

ᴄᴏ Day 1 ᴀᴗ

"I'm really having a hard time with patience lately," my friend said.

"It started with my air conditioner breaking during the hottest week of the year. I called the service place. They were swamped, but they promised to get someone out by the end of the day.

"I said I had to leave to teach a class. 'Do you want me to have someone at the house to let the repairman in?' 'No,' the guy says. 'All he has to do is go in the backyard to fix it. He doesn't need access to the house.'

"I leave to teach class, the first in a series I'm teaching at the community college. I had called and made arrangements for thirty chairs to be set up, two each at fifteen tables. I called again to make sure it was right. The guy assured me everything was fine. So I walk into my classroom and what do I see? Thirty chairs set up in a circle. No tables.

"I go to the office. I tell the guy I have to have fifteen tables. 'Fifteen tables?' he asked. He called for help. Two more guys came into the room. 'Fifteen tables?' they asked. Class was scheduled to begin in five minutes. Half an hour later, class began.

"On my way home, I had to pick up a prescription refill. I had called it in earlier. The automated voice told me my prescription would be ready in an hour. I go to the drive-through window at the pharmacy and the pharmacist says, 'We're out of that medicine. But the delivery truck should be here with it shortly. Can you come back in an hour?'

"I do errands and then return to the drive-through window. 'The truck is here but it's not unloaded yet. Can you come back in half an hour?' I bite my tongue and go kill another half hour. When I return, she says, 'Almost ready, dear. How about returning in fifteen minutes?'

"I finally got my prescription and went home. It was sweltering. I couldn't wait to get in the house and cool down. But when I turn on the air conditioner, it's still broken. I called the repair place. 'We sent someone to fix it,' the guy said. 'But nobody was home to let him in.'

"I blew," my friend said. "I couldn't bite my tongue anymore. The guy says there's nothing he can do about it now, it's too late in the day. He offered to schedule an appointment for later in the week. I told him to forget it and slammed down the phone.

"Now I'm sitting here sweating, with no air conditioning, and no appointment to get it fixed. I thought I showed him," she said. "But it occurred to me that I'm the one suffering."

"I'm not very patient," I've heard many people say, as though patience were a character trait we are either born with or without. "Patience is a virtue," others say. I think patience is a necessity, if we want to give up our self-sabotaging ways.

Value: Whether we call it a trait or virtue, the value of patience is what we'll explore this week.

७६ Day 2 ९९

"I like to get at the end of the line and push," a friend said.

Application: There are times when we take inconveniences, setbacks, and delays in stride. Patience isn't a problem. We need to practice patience the most when we're feeling stressed, blue, angry, or pressured.

७६ Day 3 ९९

We may wait and wait for life to get better, but in that instance, patience isn't the problem. Doing something differently—making changes in ourselves—is the issue at hand. We may wait and wait for someone else to change, but again, the value isn't being patient. It's letting go and changing ourselves.

It's easy to get confused about when to practice patience and when to stop waiting for something that's not going to happen. Or we may confuse being patient with not feeling our feelings. We can feel our feelings of impatience without turning them into impatient behaviors that hurt ourselves.

Challenge: The hardest thing about practicing patience is that practicing impatience feels so justified.

७६ Day 4 ९९

There is a principle of divine timing in the universe. That timing isn't always ours.

Inventory Focus: Are you open to considering the idea that the rest of the world may not be moving too slowly? Perhaps you are moving too quickly.

⟲ Day 5 ⟳

"Can you be patient?" a mother asked her two-year-old, as he demanded ice cream.

"Be patient," he said. Then he innocently turned his attention to something else.

Action: Can you be patient with the person ahead of you who wants to count out every penny for exact change? Can you be patient when traffic doesn't move as fast as you'd like? Can you be patient with newcomers in any field where you're an old-timer? Can you be patient with children and older folks? Can you be patient when people make mistakes or don't grow, change, or get it as quickly as you'd like? Can you be patient with yourself, with the fact that you're not further along than you are? Can you be patient with others and yourself as you each grind through a process in which the timing isn't necessarily ours?

I was listening to a conversation at a coffee shop one day. One man was complaining to another man about a business deal that wasn't materializing.

"You know the guy's word is good," the other man explained. "You know it's going to happen sooner or later. Can you be patient?" he said.

What are you waiting for? Can you be patient too?

໑ **Day 6** ໑

It's hard to wait. It's especially hard to wait when we're not sure we're going to get what we want. Sometimes we need to stop waiting and do something else. It might happen, or it might not. Would we even want it, if it wasn't God's Will?

Gratitude Focus: *We can be grateful for all the times people—and our Higher Power—have been patient with us.*

໑ **Day 7** ໑

I broke my finger in a sporting accident, drove to the emergency room, then left impatiently after waiting three hours and getting no medical attention. Two years later, I required a surgery that only partially repaired my injury, and it cost thousands of dollars.

"If you would have had it set when you originally broke it, it wouldn't be this bad," the doctor patiently explained.

Patience might feel like it hurts, but I have a permanently crooked finger to remind me that impatience hurts more.

Prayer: *Help me stop sabotaging myself because I'm too impatient to wait. Teach me to trust your timing, especially when it doesn't coincide with mine.*

Guidance

❧ Day 1 ❧

I explained a dilemma to a friend. "I just don't know what to do about it," I said.

"That's because you haven't been shown a solution yet," he said.

Before I could get out of treatment, I had to get a job. I scoured the town, applied for every job possible, did everything I could think of to do. Nothing opened up. Finally, after a month of job hunting, I had run out of ideas. I was standing on a corner waiting for the bus, when I heard it, clear as a bell. It was a thought, but not my own.

"Turn around."

I did. There was a stairway leading to a second-floor law firm. I had a history, tumultuous as it was, of working in law firms. But it never occurred to me to even try to get a job as a legal secretary. I was in treatment in a state hospital. I had a criminal record. Although I was making every effort to clean up my life, I didn't consider myself a desirable employee because of my past.

"Go upstairs. Ask to talk to the owner of the firm. Tell him you want a job."

"This is insane," I thought, climbing the stairs.

I talked to the owner of the firm. It turned out he had

a family member with an alcohol problem. He understood. He also said he had been thinking about hiring another secretary, but hadn't gotten around to advertising yet. Two weeks later, he called. I got the job. Not only did it pay more money than any of the other jobs I had applied for, it was better suited to my skills. This story is only one of dozens and dozens of such experiences where divine guidance helped me take important steps in my life.

Divine guidance may come as a message from a friend. It may be inspired by a book, movie, or TV show. It may be an idea that quietly occurs to us. Sometimes it's as simple as sorting out the next small step to take. Or it may be more vivid, almost as though the angels are talking directly to us.

Value: Asking for and accepting guidance—and trusting it to be there for us when we need it—is the value this week.

ᢍ Day 2 ᢌ

A friend was experiencing some financial difficulties. He was getting to the point of despair. "I don't know what to do," he said.

"Why don't you ask God?" I said.

"I couldn't do that. I've already asked God too many times to bail me out."

"I don't mean ask God to bail you out," I said. "Ask God to show you what to do."

"I never thought of that," he said.

We all have access to the greatest resource in the world. We don't have to sign up, register, or pay dues. Wherever we are, whatever we're facing, all we need to do is ask our

Higher Power what to do next. Why is it that the simplest things in life can be the hardest things to do?

Application: Got financial problems? Relationship problems? Facing a quandary in life? Stepping into the vast wilderness called the unknown? *If we've run out of our own answers, it is time to ask for guidance. Or better yet, we can ask for guidance* before *running out of our own resources. Asking for guidance—for knowledge of God's Will for us and the power to carry that out—is a good thing to do as needed and each day.*

✧ Day 3 ✧

I'll admit it. I do forget to ask for guidance—until I've worn myself out. Or I take action before I seek guidance. And when I find myself in the midst of a mess, asking for guidance doesn't occur to me. We all do this and it is understandable, considering that to survive, we may have had to figure things out on our own, because we could not depend on others.

There have been times when I felt that guidance has gotten me into a mess; other times I feel that self-will has. When my son died, I was so angry at God that I didn't want to ask for guidance. Not only did I not want the problem, I didn't want guidance getting through it.

It's always appropriate to ask God what to do next, whether we're in the midst of a mess, or headed toward one; whether we feel like we've created the mess, or the problem is too petty to solve. It's especially wise to ask God for guidance when we're all alone, with no help, and feel abandoned by God too.

Challenge: For me, the hardest thing about guidance is that no matter how many times I've asked for guidance and received it, I'm always afraid it won't be there for me in the future. We need to remember we're never alone.

✌ Day 4 ✌

A friend has a cat that likes to drag chipmunks into the house to play. I called my friend one day when he was in the midst of a frenzy. "The cat brought another chipmunk in. He brings it in, drops it in my office. The chipmunk freaks out, starts running up my leg, realizes what he's done, then everyone goes berserk. Now one of them—I think it was the cat—just crashed into the window and broke it."

Sometimes we all panic, but panic doesn't help. Guidance does.

Inventory Focus: Are you panicking because of some problem in your life? Does the problem seem unsolvable? Don't panic. If you are, take a deep breath. If you don't know what to do next, it's because you haven't been shown—yet.

✌ Day 5 ✌

There is a way through everything.

Action: Ask for guidance. Then wait patiently and calmly. Be open to the answer coming in many shapes and forms. A friend may call. You may get an idea. There is so much power in asking, because asking the question opens our heart to the answer. Don't overlook the simple steps. There is a lot of power in simple solutions. Discover what feels right to you. Sometimes the silliest solution—a smile, a willing attitude—will move mountains.

⌇ **Day 6** ⌇

When we ask for guidance and knowledge of God's Will, we may not get the answer we want, but we will always get an answer.

Gratitude Focus: *We can be grateful that if we ask for the right thought, word, or action, we'll be given it. We can be grateful that whether we know it or not, we* are *being guided all along.*

⌇ **Day 7** ⌇

An acquaintance was diagnosed with incurable cancer during a national tragedy. He called his mother. "I suppose God's too busy now to care about me," he said.

She told him, "God is busy, but never too busy to care about each of us."

Prayer: *Higher Power, please show me what to do next. Then help me relax and trust that you'll guide me.*

Sweet Surrender

ᏉᏇ **Day 1** ᏏᏇ

So we're ready to take on the world, at least to take the next step. That's when it hits. Or rather we hit it.

The wall.

Suddenly the path that looked so clear, so easy, so laid out in front of us disappears. "Just a little glitch," we think. We take another run at it.

It's still there.

"Must be me," we think. "I'll try a little harder. Get this problem under control." We may mumble a few words to a Higher Power, something about needing help, but essentially we're praying for enough steam to ram into and run through that wall, sometimes chanting the mantra "My will be done" all the way.

"What I want is good and right," we tell ourselves. "I've just got to keep at it."

I wish I could tell you there is a way to avoid this wall-banging, head-bumping vortex of chaos, but if there is, I haven't found it.

It's a dirty dust devil of self-will.

Hearing that we're powerless over people, places, and things (such as alcohol and other drugs)—intellectually understanding that concept—is one thing. Experiencing powerlessness is another.

I didn't surrender to my powerlessness over alcohol and drugs because I wanted to. I surrendered because I had to, because I was worn out, because I couldn't keep going anymore. I went down hard.

I finally surrendered to my inability to control the alcoholism of someone I loved, not because it seemed like the right thing to do. It was the only thing left to do.

I didn't surrender to my son's death because I wanted to. I had no choice.

When I first learned about surrendering, it seemed impossible. Now, when I'm not in that surrendered place, it still seems foreign and faraway.

One morning, a friend called to see whether I had solved a problem I was struggling with.

"Yup," I said. "I told God last night that whatever happened was okay with me, I was willing to do whatever he wanted. And I meant it."

"Oh that," she said gently. "Sweet surrender."

"Yeah," I said. "It's sweet . . . now."

Surrender. The place that those of us on a spiritual path call home.

Not only is it sweet, there's no place like it, as Dorothy told us in *The Wizard of Oz*.

Value: Whether we call it surrendering control, surrendering to God's Will, getting out of our own way, powerlessness, or running out of ourselves, that's this week's value.

✎ **Day 2** ✎

It's not always life's big events—change, loss, or illness—that overpower us. Sometimes engaging in battle with the smaller realities—those tasks we think we should be able to accomplish on our own, small problems or decisions, irritating financial problems—can wear us out.

"I give myself a migraine headache unless I start each day by getting down on my knees and surrendering to God's Will," a friend said.

Application: Surrender is a helpful value to practice daily. Whenever we tell ourselves we should be able to do something and we can't, whenever we're giving ourselves a headache from spinning our wheels trying to figure something out and we can't, it may be time to officially wave the white flag. If we find ourselves urgently trying to make something happen by sheer will, surrender may be the value we need to apply.

✎ **Day 3** ✎

"I'm not going to bed tonight until I figure this out," a friend proclaimed one day. She was going through a lot of change, and she was scared. "I'm going to research fear and try to understand why I'm going through this," she said.

"While you're at it," I said, "why don't you research surrender too."

There's a lot of hard parts to surrendering. We may feel like we have to, should, or can do it ourselves. We may not like feeling the emotions involved with losing something that's important to us. Many of us are head-dwellers, and it's hard to get out of that space and into our emotions. Or surrendering may involve change, bringing with it the uncertainty of not knowing what's coming next or admitting we don't know what to do now. It's hard to give up our ideas about how things should be, how they should go, or how we planned them to go. We may have a difficult time being vulnerable with people we can hear and see, so surrendering to a Power we can't see can be a real stretch.

Challenge: *The hardest part of surrendering is remembering to do it.*

✑ Day 4 ✑

"How are you today," the young man behind the counter at the fast–food chicken shack asked.

"Not good," I said.

"What's the matter?" he said.

I didn't know what the matter was. Later I would see that I had spent the last week caught in that nasty vortex of self-will, trying to *figure something out,* plow ahead, and ram through that wall. I wasn't trying to control anything that big, but the battle had grown to monstrous proportions. How could I tell this young man that I was suffering from battle fatigue when I wasn't even aware of it myself?

"I'm just a little out of it," I said.

What I was *out of* was that gentle place called *God's Will.* What I wasn't out of yet was *myself.*

He handed me my chicken.

"I hope you're on your way home," he said.

I was. I surrendered that night.

Inventory Focus: *Have you had any past experiences with surrender? How has that worked for you? Are you* *struggling with an issue right now and losing? Is there a person, place, or thing in your life that you're trying to control? How's that working for you? Like the young man said to me, I hope you're on your way home.*

～ Day 5 ～

"Get out of your own way." "Just surrender control." "You can't do anything about it, so stop trying." Well-meaning friends may see what our problem is—even if we can't—and give us wise advice.

My standard reply is "How?"

Surrendering control isn't like riding a bicycle, at least not for me. I have to learn it anew each time I do it.

Action: *Surrendering means doing nothing about whatever you can't do anything about. Try not to stare at it either. Do something else, something you can do. Try to relax, just a little. If you must do something, say "Thy will be done" and mean it.*

～ Day 6 ～

It's kind of nice to know we're not in this thing alone.

Gratitude Focus: *Instead of beating our head against the wall, let's practice gratitude for all the situations that are irritating us—exactly as they are. Thank God we're not in control and that there's a plan other than ours. If we can't bring ourselves to practice or express gratitude for the circumstance, then we can at least practice gratitude for how we're feeling about it. The idea is to move from resistance to serenity.*

ᶜᵛ Day 7 ᵛᵘ

See how good it feels to be finally home?

See how magical and interesting life can be when we get out of our way? And out of God's way?

We can be peaceful at last.

There's a place in each of us that's connected to God. Surrendering control helps us relax into it.

Prayer: *Higher Power, help me remember that I'm not giving up anything by surrendering to your will. That's how I find true strength.*

Presence

⟿ Day 1 ⟾

"I wonder what's wrong," I said, trying to describe the morass I was in to a friend. "It feels like I'm wandering through a swamp wearing concrete boots."

"Silly girl," she said. "Nothing's wrong. God just doesn't want you to miss anything."

Well, there's a lot of things in my life I wouldn't have minded missing. Let's start with my childhood: being molested and blacking out at age thirteen from my alcoholism. I could have done without those things.

Then there was that stabbing pain in my heart when I realized that someone I loved was lying to me, and the years of loneliness while I was a single parent to my two children.

There is nothing I wouldn't do to have missed the words of that nurse in the hospital after my son Shane's accident: "Do you have someone you can call? I'm sorry, there's no hope." During the years that followed, my feelings vacillated between numbness, rage at God, and overwhelming sadness.

But here's the problem. If I would have missed out on those things, I would have missed out on some other things, things I wouldn't have missed for the world: the deep bond I have with my daughter, from the years we spent together in our little single-parent family; the self-esteem and independence I got from raising my family on my own; the compassion that was worked into me from not getting what I wanted as a child; the twelve years I got to spend with my son, Shane. I can still remember what it felt like when he brushed my cheek with a kiss.

It's not that you take the good with the bad. It runs deeper than that. The good, the bad, and the in-between start to run together and become inseparable. Together, they paint the picture of a life. We can't create a good scrapbook unless we can remember what happened. We can't remember it if we weren't there.

Slow down. Be present. No, not that gaze-into-someone's-eyes, needy-codependent thing. Just be there. Where you are.

The magic isn't tomorrow or in some far-off place. The magic is in the moment and the exact details of the situation we're in right now.

Value: *"Hurry-worry never works," said Tsung Tsai in* Bones of the Master. *This week we'll practice being present for ourselves, our emotions, other people, God, work, and life.*

ᴄᴠᴀ Day 2 ᴀᴠᴅ

Recovery programs and religions teach many of us to live one day at a time. When my son died, even one day at a time was too much.

"Just stay present for each feeling," a friend suggested one day. "If you're numb, be numb. If you're sad, cry. If you're overwhelmed, be overwhelmed."

Being fully present for each emotion—and for each moment—isn't just a grief-survival tool. It's a practical and valuable way to live life.

Application: Being present may be particularly useful when we are going through a difficult time, dreading what we are going through, not knowing what's coming next, or starting something new. It's also helpful when we find ourselves moving too fast, overly distracted, worried, anxious, overly focused on outcomes, living in the future or the past—or when we find ourselves inconvenienced by wearing those concrete boots.

༄ Day 3 ༄

Most of us want what we don't have, including being somewhere other than where we are. "Someplace else would be better," we think. Sometimes we're not present because we genuinely don't like where we are or whom we're with—and being present would bring that reality home. Fear, anxiety, guilt, and other unresolved emotions from the past can block our ability to be present now.

Living in the present moment doesn't just mean showing up and thinking. It involves slowing down and moving down, into our heart.

Challenge: The hardest part about being here now, wherever that is, is that sometimes it hurts. The good thing about it is, if we're present for each emotion, we'll be present when joy comes around too.

༄ Day 4 ༄

"AndthankyouforkeepingmestraightyesterdayAmen."

Sometimes I can almost hear God saying, "What did she just say?"

Inventory Focus: *Are you rushing through or skipping prayer and meditation time? Are people in your life asking where you are, even though you're in the room with them when they ask? Are you so focused on an outcome that you've forgotten to enjoy each step along the way? Do you have so many things to do that you're doing them all at once and not getting anything done? We receive from life what we put in, unless we're pouring our energy into a black hole. Are you getting what you want out of your relationships, work, and leisure time? How much of you are you investing?*

ᴄᴍ Day 5 ᴍᴄ

"C'mon. Hurry. Let's go," my friend said, shifting nervously from one foot to the other.

I looked around. Another friend, Michael, had just walked into the room. I hadn't seen him for a while. I felt compelled to go over and talk to him, even though I didn't have anything important to say.

"Please, let's go," my friend said again. I started to leave with him, then changed my mind.

"Give me just a few minutes," I said, walking away from my friend and moving toward Michael. We didn't talk about much, Michael and I. But I'll never forget that conversation. He was killed in an accident two weeks later.

Some people suggest that our biggest regret, when we die, will be that we didn't work less and spend more time with the people we love. That may be true, but for me, I think it will be that I wasn't more completely present for each person, task, and moment in my life.

Action: Do you remember the "stop, look, and, listen" slogan from when you were a child? Every so often, even for a few minutes each day, try to remember to practice it.

Slow down or stop, depending on how fast you're going.

Look. See where you are, whom you're with, what you're doing. Give whatever you're doing your attention.

Listen. As much as possible, quell your anxiety, cease your mental chatter, and just listen to nature, to other people, to God, and to yourself.

ᏯᎾ Day 6 ᎠᏋ

Being present breeds gratitude. The more present we are for each moment of our lives, the more gratitude we'll feel.

Gratitude Focus: Being present for each detail of our lives is a way of showing gratitude.

ᏯᎾ Day 7 ᎠᏋ

Did you ever receive an invitation that began with "Your presence is requested"? Well, you just got another one. Your presence is hereby requested in your life.

Prayer: Higher Power, please help me see the beauty of my life.

An Open Heart

❧ Day 1 ❧

Take everything with a grain of salt. Watch your back. Don't trust just anyone, especially someone who says, "Trust me, baby, I know what I'm doing." Be skeptical. Check it out. Trust your gut.

Words of wisdom.

Who wants to be anybody's fool, especially in a world where people mistake kindness for weakness, or worse yet, for stupidity?

I was riding in a car with a friend when we passed a homeless woman strategically positioned by an intersection. She was displaying an elaborate multicolored sign asking for money. I asked, "If she's so broke, where'd she get money for colored markers?"

More than once, I've seen this friend stick a dollar— or five—in a beggar's hand and gently say, "God bless you." And mean it. My friend, now happily married with two children and a promising career in the arts, explained why. Years ago, she had lived in a big city. That's where she had gotten into recovery for her own addiction to alcohol and other drugs.

"I was lost," she said. "I didn't believe I could get sober. I was using so much cocaine, it's a miracle I'm still alive. The way I was living was . . . disgusting. But I couldn't stop.

"I decided to attend a meeting of Alcoholics Anonymous. I was so confused, I didn't even feel like I belonged there. Then this one guy befriended me. I felt safe with him. He'd sit by me at meetings. He called a couple times each day. Sometimes he even stopped by my apartment and walked me to a meeting, just to make sure I'd go. He never did anything out of line. His friendship was a big factor in saving my life. I'm not sure I would have kept going to those meetings, especially in the beginning, if it hadn't been for him.

"He was a nice guy and had been clean from drugs for some time. But about the time recovery started kicking in for me, he started using heroin again. I couldn't believe it at first. He avoided my calls. Then he just disappeared. One day, I saw this beggar. He was all dirty and disgusting, sitting up against the wall, with a tin cup in front of him.

"I looked more closely. He was so out of it he didn't recognize me, but I knew him. It was the guy who helped save my life. I'll never look at a beggar or a homeless person the same way again," my friend said. "It could be me someday. Or it could be someone who saves my life—or the life of someone I love."

How do we stay unjaded in a cynical world? The answer to that question isn't any easier than doing it. We do the best we can.

Value: Some people call it not becoming jaded. *Others call it* staying open. *A few brave souls actually say the words* opening our heart. *Call it whatever makes you comfortable. That's the value we'll practice this week.*

ᖰᖰ **Day 2** ᖰᖰ

When I looked up *jaded* in the dictionary, I was surprised to learn that it doesn't mean cynical, bizarre, or hardened. Jaded means bored, tired, overexposed, and exhausted.

It's understandable that we shut down. It's a protective response to too much pain. But after a while, being closed becomes boring. Too much exposure to anything—even something that's good—can cause us to shut down. Balance is the key.

> ***Application:*** *It's time to "unjade" ourselves when we find ourselves preaching to people instead of sharing honestly, when we haven't felt anything except irritated and tired for a long time, when we've just been through one or a series of incidents where we've had to protect ourselves, when we lose our sense of wonder and awe.*

ᖰᖰ **Day 3** ᖰᖰ

"It's hard to wake up every day and live life with passion and an open heart," my daughter said.

The hardest thing about staying open, for me, is getting back into my heart after I've shut down to survive. Feeling whatever made me want to shut down is a challenge too. Taking care of myself while I'm open is tough. I either get so soft and mushy that I'm an easy target, or I turn into a pit bull. Or sometimes I just get scared of being that vulnerable. I wear myself out, running back and forth between my head and my heart.

I am also an extremist, eagerly overexposing myself to anything, including the good things in life. Everything about staying open challenges me.

Challenge: What is the hardest thing about staying open?

ལྕ Day 4 ལྩ

It is normal to not want to be *that open* all the time. There are times we need to back off, go a little numb. Knowing that we can protect ourselves is an important part of staying open. But we don't need to put so much armor around our heart that it takes a battering ram to get back in.

Inventory Focus: How do you protect yourself when you become exposed, even potentially, to pain, disappointment, or manipulation? Do you make a decision never to be open again? Are you willing to open up, even a little?

ལྕ Day 5 ལྩ

Get out in nature. Go to a heart-opening movie. Spend time with a favorite friend. If you're in recovery, go to a meeting. Hold a baby, pet a puppy, or listen to some of your favorite music. Do something nice for someone or let someone do something nice for you. Do something that helps you believe in life again.

The danger in becoming jaded is that we can easily become cynical about the very things that help us enjoy life.

Action: Make a list of activities that help you stay open. Then pick one of the things on your list and do it. Then do another. If you have been exposed to too much pain, try exposing yourself to something that feels good, safe, fun, and comfortable.

If you have been exposed to too much of anything, try exposing yourself to something else.

⋙ **Day 6** ⋘

It's easy to become cynical. Unjading ourselves is a choice.

Gratitude Focus: *We can be grateful for all the people, places, and activities that help us open our heart.*

⋙ **Day 7** ⋘

"I've seen you go through this process so many times," a friend remarked. "You go numb. Then you get angry. Then you cry. Then you settle down and you're gentle, sweet, and vulnerable again."

Don't force it. Opening our heart a little can go a long way.

You will discover how the world looks through eyes of love. It's like the difference between looking at a flat picture, then seeing the same scene in 3-D. It's the same place, only nicer.

Prayer: *Higher Power, please protect me. Please send me exactly what I need to stay in my heart. It's hard to go there. Please take my hands, show me where to go, what to say, and how to love.*

Good Grief

ᴄᴏ Day 1 ᴄᴏ

"The strangest thing happened," said my friend, a lovably neurotic, *very* obsessive businessman in his midforties.

"I was watching one of those afternoon TV talk shows. This one was about problem kids. A parent comes on. She talks about how out of control her child is. Then a parenting expert comes on. He does tough love with the kids, like a drill sergeant, screaming and getting in their faces. Then he takes the troubled kids for a week and straightens them out.

"So this nine-year-old boy comes on. He's been a monster. Killing animals in the neighborhood. Driving his mother nuts. The drill sergeant guy gets right up in this kid's face. He's screaming. 'You think you're tough? You're a tough guy?'

"The expert's screaming at the kid. The kid is just standing there. And I'm watching this thinking, 'Maybe this kid is just a bad seed.'

"'How'd you like me to come home with you for a week? Be in your face like this all the time,' the expert hollered. 'Would you like that?'

"'Yes,' the boy said.

" 'What did you say? Yes? You'd like that? Why would you like that?'

" 'Because I don't have a dad,' " the kid said. The boy's lip quivered. The expert got silent. The audience went nuts. But that's not the strange thing," my friend said. "Melody, I started crying. Sobbing like a baby. I haven't cried for ten years."

"What do you think that was about?" I asked.

"I realized how much I missed having a dad," he said. "When people asked me, I always said it wasn't important. I didn't know until I saw that show and started crying that you could miss something you never had."

Sometimes we don't know what or whom we're missing.

"How can I stop feeling so blue about being separated from my children?" another friend asked when business had taken him away from home for a month.

"You're asking the wrong person," I said. "It has been eleven years since my son died, and I still miss him every day."

Grief. It may strike suddenly, catching our heart by surprise. Or it may pound relentlessly and persistently for years, like ocean waves beating on the shore.

Whether we're conscious of what or whom we're missing, our heart knows. We may never be happy about whom or what we have lost, but it is possible to be happy again.

Value: Grief isn't an abnormal condition. It's nature's way of healing our heart. And that's the value this week.

✎ Day 2 ✎

We don't *do* grief. Grief *does* us.

Application: Don't worry about when this value applies. When it's time to heal our heart from a loss, we'll know. Don't be surprised if grief hits years after a loss, or takes longer than we think it should.

∽ Day 3 ∾

Few of us like to feel sad or cry. Grief can be tricky. Elisabeth Kübler-Ross identified the five stages of grief: denial, anger, bargaining, depression, and acceptance. Those words barely convey the shock that can leave us dazed and numb for months, or the white-hot rage many of us feel, often toward our Higher Power, when we lose someone we love, or the odd way we feel so separated from the rest of the world when we grieve.

Then there are the stages of grief that few people discuss: the obsession with what we've lost, the guilt that's part of grief ("I could have prevented it"), and the way grief can play havoc with our self-esteem ("I must be a terrible person for this to happen to me").

People may say stupid things like "Aren't you over that yet?" You may even expect yourself to be healed from a loss long before your heart is ready.

Challenge: Nothing about grief is easy. We may have to live with the pain from some losses all our lives. But the hardest thing for many people is losing the person they love.

We may think that being healed means we don't miss that person anymore. What it really means is we're willing to move forward with our lives.

✒ **Day 4** ✒

Some cultures mandate a formal time of grief for people. I think we should wear big badges when we're grieving that say "Fragile. Heart under construction. Handle with care."

> ***Inventory Focus:*** *Are you going through loss or change? Are you missing someone due to physical separation, a change in the relationship, or death? Can you be gentle and respectful with yourself and others in times of loss and change?*

✒ **Day 5** ✒

It was years after my son's death. I was functioning pretty well by then. I was happy to be alive, enjoying my life. But then one of those grief waves came splashing over me, catching me by surprise.

I needed to go to the grocery store, but I couldn't get motivated. Once there, I couldn't figure out whether to use a large shopping cart or one of those smaller baskets. I chose the basket. Then I put that down; I only needed a few things.

I walked down the aisles, trying to carry everything in my arms. I kept dropping things and wasn't able to pick them back up.

After I returned home, the wave eventually subsided, and I called a friend. I talked, she listened. There wasn't much else for me to do.

> ***Action:*** *If a sudden wave of sadness hits, feel whatever you feel. If you are going through an extended grief process, don't expect normal functioning from yourself.*

Go into survival mode. Put together an emergency-care kit: music, phone numbers of best friends, favorite movies, anything that helps you get through the moments.

When your grief gets too intense, write a letter to the person you miss. Put it in a special place and ask God to deliver the message. Learn to honor this process of healing your hurts.

✺ Day 6 ✺

If you find yourself swimming across an ocean of grief, and you're too tired to keep swimming, just float.

Gratitude Focus: *We can be thankful that we don't have to accept our losses, or the magnitude of each loss, all at once. All we need to accept is whatever we're feeling today.*

✺ Day 7 ✺

A woman gave me a sculpture. It was a heart that had once been broken in several places but had been pieced together. I thanked her for the message: A broken heart, once healed, is a work of art.

Prayer: *Higher Power, hold me close when I feel sad and miss someone or something. Help me remember that each wave of sadness washes away the old and washes in the new. Teach me compassion. Show me how to comfort myself and others.*

Serenity

ᘉᕗ Day 1 ᘏᕬ

Your body is tense. Your face is somber and serious, ready to *deliver the news.* You may be slightly breathless. There's a crisis. It may be real. Or it may be self-created.

Like an audience in a sports arena, we watch the events of life—or even The Weather Channel—drumming up reactive responses. Fear. Sometimes panic. "Oh my God, what if . . ."

I called my daughter in this frame of mind one morning, ready to report on the latest current event in my life. I barely had three words out of my mouth when she interrupted me.

"You're talking in your drama-addiction tone."

"God, grant me the serenity to accept the things I cannot change, the courage to change the things I can, and the wisdom to know the difference." I've probably said this prayer out loud a thousand times, and silently twice that amount. It's called the Serenity Prayer, not the Courage Prayer, not the Wisdom Prayer. That is because, no matter what we're doing, before we receive courage or wisdom, serenity needs to come first.

I recall talking to a friend during the height of my drama-addiction years. If possible, he thrived on drama more than I. We were discussing our problem with drama addiction and possible solutions.

"When I think about living without drama, everything just seems so plain, so boring," I said.

"I know," he said. "I'm just not sure I'm ready to let that addiction go."

Value: Serenity is the value for this week. Don't panic. And if we do, we can make it a priority to calm ourselves before we do anything else.

ᏯᏣ Day 2 ᏯᏣ

Panic is contagious. So is serenity. It's just a little harder to catch.

Application: Whenever our emotions are churning and we're trying to function from a base of anxiety and panic, serenity is a good value to apply. When we find ourselves trying to convince someone else they should be upset, it may be time to convince ourselves to get calm.

ᏯᏣ Day 3 ᏯᏣ

I was standing in line to pay my bill at a restaurant. The woman in line ahead of me wrote out a check to pay her bill, then handed the cashier her driver's license. The cashier looked at the license.

"Is everything current?" she asked the woman.

The woman sighed. "For twenty-two years," she said. She turned to me and added, "I'm so boring."

That's not serenity. It's boredom. And there's a difference.

Serenity doesn't mean we stick our head in the sand, don't interact with life, or don't feel our legitimate emotions. Serenity is a deliberate decision to practice a calm, serene attitude, despite our problems and emotions.

Challenge: *The most difficult part about practicing serenity can be getting past our fear that we'll sink into a life of boredom if we're not churning with drama. Even if the problem is real and not self-created, sustained turmoil doesn't help. Urgency and panic feed on themselves, and they can make us feel like the correct response is to become more urgent, more panicked. Turmoil can actually block or delay solving the problem. Or it can keep us from identifying and solving our real problem, such as why we're so bored with our lives.*

Serenity isn't boring. Drama addiction is. We can create a fulfilling life without creating a crisis.

༒ Day 4 ༒

"I'm all panicked. I don't know what to do next," a friend explained. "I've been praying all night asking God what to do so I can calm down."

"What did God say?" I asked.

"I don't know," my friend said. "I'm so full of anxiety I can't hear."

Inventory Focus: *Do you need a crisis to feel alive? Are you experiencing a real problem that's causing you to feel anxious? Are you waiting for the arrival of a solution in order to calm you, rather than practicing serenity? Have you been trying to solve your problem first, before calming down? How's that working? If anxiety isn't helping, calming yourself may be the first problem you need to solve.*

⟳ **Day 5** ⟲

"I was lucky," a man explained to me. "One of my first mentors in life made me practice serenity. Whenever I'd call him in full-blown panic mode or with that frantic tone in my voice, he'd refuse to talk to me until I calmed myself down.

"'Go get centered,' he'd tell me. 'Then we'll talk.'"

Sometimes we need help working through our panic, anxiety, and fear. Find someone to talk to who will support serenity, rather than feed anxiety. Learn to recognize turmoil and urgency in your body, speech, emotions, and thought. Learn what it feels like to be centered and calm.

Practicing serenity is a learned behavior and an art.

Action: When you find yourself in turmoil, stop what you are doing. Take deliberate steps to relax. Talk to a friend, say the Serenity Prayer or any favorite prayer, breathe, meditate, feel any emotions you need to feel. Calming yourself may feel awkward at first, nearly impossible. (Some people may need professional help to deal with anxiety and panic, if it's chronic and continual.) Over time and with practice, you will discover ways to calm yourself, the way a loving parent learns to calm a fretting child.

⟳ **Day 6** ⟲

Practicing serenity doesn't mean we're *always* calm and serene. It means we remember to practice serenity whenever we feel unrest.

Gratitude Focus: There are a lot of events, people, and circumstances in the world that help us feel chaotic. We can be grateful for all the people, places, and things that help promote peace.

～ **Day 7** ～

Oh, I see. God didn't promise a life free from problems. God promised peace if we put our trust in him.

Prayer: *Serenity and peace are great gifts. Higher Power, help me remember to accept these gifts. Show each of us how much better life is when lived through these blessings.*

Passion

ⳝ **Day 1** ⳝ

The *cupcake thing* started the summer of 2002.

"Come to New York," my daughter Nichole insisted. "We'll go to the park, go shopping. And you've got to try these cupcakes I've discovered," she said. "Fluffy, white, vanilla cake. You can choose the color frosting you want: blue, green, yellow. It's just a tiny bakery," she said. "But those cupcakes. You can smell them a block away."

"A block away?" I thought. After a few conversations, I could smell them across the country in my California home.

"They sell thousands of cupcakes each day," Nichole said. "Some people need their cupcake fix so bad they have a fit if they can't get the color they like."

"Mail me some," I said.

"I can't," Nichole said. "They'll melt."

I couldn't stop thinking about those cupcakes. I started telling friends about them. And I hadn't even tasted them yet.

"You're driving me nuts," a friend in Minnesota said. "After our last conversation, I drove to my neighborhood bakery, bought two cupcakes, then went out to my car and ate them—right there in the parking lot. Would you stop with the cupcake thing?" she asked.

I couldn't.

I had a break in my schedule, so I decided to visit New York for the Fourth of July. When I arrived at my hotel, Nichole called and asked what I wanted to do. I only had two days in the city.

"Get cupcakes," I said.

"I think they close early today," she said. "It's a holiday tomorrow."

"Then let's run," I said.

We made it to the bakery thirty minutes before closing. I walked down the street, oblivious to everything except the vanilla cake with butter-cream frosting melting in my mouth. It was as good as I had fantasized.

Maybe better.

I called my friend in Minnesota.

"Mail me some," she begged.

"Can't," I said. "They'll melt."

The summer ended. My daughter returned to Los Angeles. She called one afternoon to invite me to a barbeque.

"What are you doing?" she asked.

"Baking cupcakes," I said. By then, I had a copy of the bakery's cookbook, which included the recipe for cupcakes. I had passed the recipe to Minnesota friends. They had fallen in love with them too. I brought the cupcakes to the barbeque.

"These are the best cupcakes I've ever eaten," one guest commented.

The Magnolia Bakery in New York was started by a group of people who were dissatisfied with their lives, quit their jobs, and decided to do something they had a passion for: baking.

A little passion can go a long way.

Don't be so quick to judge everything as obsession. Don't be afraid of that fire in your heart. Sure, we run the risk of getting obsessed. And sometimes we go to extremes. But passion makes life more interesting and fun. Passion is the secret to almost every success story I've heard.

Value: Passion is the value this week.

✍ Day 2 ✍

"Write a lead that inspires me. Find the passion in the story," an editor at a daily paper goaded so long ago.

She taught me a valuable lesson. I didn't have to write high-drama stories about murders or election nights to find passion. I could cover a city-council meeting or a cheer-leading competition and find something to be interested in if I listen to people and to my heart.

Has life gotten dull, boring, lackluster? Maybe you need a new life with new goals and new dreams. Or maybe you just need to awaken your passion for the people, places, and things already in your life.

Application: We all go through the motions at times, but if we're constantly bored, unenthusiastic, and disinterested in life, passion may be the value to apply. If we're creating a lot of artificial drama, we can light a real fire in our heart by finding out what we're passionate about. We may not need to change our lives. We may just need to take a risk and learn what genuinely interests us.

ᴄᴡ **Day 3** ᴡᴄ

Sometimes people have judged my passions as unnecessary obsessions. Sometimes they are. I have been asked, "Why can't you just go to Al-Anon meetings instead of constantly talking about codependency?" Was it obsession? Or passion? Probably both. But my passion for the subject turned into a book that changed my life.

It can be easier to go numb and stay in denial than to feel all the emotions we feel when we're fully alive. Living passionately does rock the proverbial boat.

> **Challenge:** *The hardest part about living passionately is that we may think it's wrong to follow our heart. "I should do what others expect me to do," we think. "That's what God wants me to do." Usually when we follow our heart, even when we're afraid it's wrong, it turns out to be exactly what we need to do.*

ᴄᴡ **Day 4** ᴡᴄ

"This week, I went scuba diving," a man told me. "Hadn't done it for years. I forgot how much doing something I love, even for one afternoon, can change my entire outlook on life."

It's easy to tell ourselves we can't have what we want and can't do what we want. And sometimes, we can't. But once in a while, even for an afternoon, it is helpful to treat yourself.

> **Inventory Focus:** *How long has it been since you did something you loved? Are you willing to be open to what excites and inspires you? If you can't do what you love, can you find passion in what you are doing?*

❧ Day 5 ❧

"Stomp. Scream. Spit. Cry," a friend said. "Just don't go numb again. Maybe what you're really angry about is that you've been dead longer than Abe Lincoln, and now you're finally coming back to life."

There's a price to pay for passion. We need to feel our emotions.

Action: Pay attention to how you feel: what you love, dislike, hate, enjoy. Pay attention to what grabs your heart, what interests you. Discover who you are, not who you think you should be.

❧ Day 6 ❧

"I never intended to be successful. Never intended to be a millionaire," said a man who has been extremely successful. "I just wanted to do something I had a passion to do."

Some of us have more fire than others. Some people will follow their hearts and become wildly and visibly successful. Others will be successful in quieter ways, gaining success that comes, at the end of the day, from being true to themselves.

Gratitude Focus: As hard as we may try to think our way through life, passion doesn't come from the head. We can be grateful for our emotions and inner longings.

❧ Day 7 ❧

We don't have to play with fire. But we can get close enough to it to warm our heart.

Prayer: *Please send me what I need to come fully alive. Show me how interesting life—and your Will—can be. Teach me to balance discipline with passion. Keep my life warm and lived from the heart.*

Service

ஒன் **Day 1** ஸ்ஸ்

"Can you serve yourself?" I asked a friend who stopped by for dinner.

"No problem," he joked. "Being self-serving is something I do well."

Serving others was first handed to me as a lifeline in early sobriety. I was in treatment for drug addiction, and people told me that if I want to help myself, I need to get involved in activities that serve others. I needed—at least for a few minutes each day—to forget about myself and think about someone else. It seemed odd to me that when there was so much to worry about in my own life, I needed to extend myself to others.

"If I don't think about me, who will?" I wondered.

A pattern began to emerge. If I engaged in activities that served others, life began to respond lovingly to what I needed too. The right thought, word, or action appeared. The right people, mentors, and helpers also appeared along the way. The right job showed up, sometimes a much better job than I would have thought I deserved.

Later, I got tangled up in this lifeline. I needed to back off from service for a while and get clear about what felt right to give. I tried to serve in impossible ways. I tried to make people stop doing things they didn't want to stop doing. I lost my clarity on what I was doing and why.

When my son died, I didn't have anything to give. I thought, "Why help others, why serve them, if I can never have what I want in life and if this pain is my reward?" That experience was necessary to my grief—the cocooning, the backing off, the healing of my own wounds. But there came a time when I wanted a life again. And the only way to get a life was to give and to serve.

With all its pitfalls and lessons, service isn't just a value that can help in our lives. It's a value that can open up miraculous possibilities.

Value: *Serving others, in a way that respects them and us, is the value for this week.*

༈ **Day 2** ༈

"You've got to give it away to keep it." That's a slogan many of us have heard. The truth about service may run deeper than that. Sometimes we've got to give it away in order to get it in the first place.

Application: *Whenever we are thinking too deeply and too hard about ourselves, it may be time to focus on doing something that serves somebody else.*

༈ **Day 3** ༈

When we're wrapped up in what others need, we may lose our self-esteem and our sense of what we need. Remember, genuine thoughtful service always respects both the giver and the receiver.

There's a danger of serving in ways that don't help, ways that foster other people's dependency on us, and ways that diminish others' ability to take responsibility for themselves. There's also a danger of hiding behind service, using our helpfulness and concern with others to avoid taking responsibility for our own lives.

It's difficult not to use service as a means to selfish ends. By serving, we get a life. We open up the gateway to receiving more and more ourselves. But if we start focusing only on what we're getting by giving, the entire circle collapses.

Service isn't a way to manipulate God or other people into giving us what we want. Service is a value to be cherished for its own sake.

Challenge: Sometimes the easiest thing to give is our money, and the hardest thing to give is ourselves.

ᕯ Day 4 ᕲ

"I'm not going to go work at the Goodwill," a man insisted one day. "That's where I draw the line with this service thing."

"I don't think anybody said you have to," I replied.

It's not just service that counts. It's service with a smile. Do what feels right to you. But maybe push yourself a little.

Inventory Focus: Are you engaged in activities that truly benefit others, even if it's something as simple as making someone a sandwich? Does what you do add to others' quality of life? Sometimes it's not what you do as much as how you do it. Are you doing something that looks like it serves others but doing it resentfully, carelessly, or with an attitude of WIIFM (what's in it for me)?

"I used to make every decision based on what's in

this for me," a man said to me. *"I finally learned that the less there is for me, the more there really is for me—in whatever I'm trying to do."*

✑ Day 5 ✑

"I'm just a hairstylist," the woman said to me almost apologetically. "I want to do something big, something important in the world."

"Do you have any idea how important it is to people to get a good haircut?" I asked.

Maybe we don't have to do anything different to be of service. We just need to bring an attitude of service to what we already do.

Action: Do one thing each day that serves someone else, with no thought of receiving anything in return. It doesn't have to be a big thing. Call someone; give them encouragement. Or just listen, instead of talking, during a conversation. Wait on someone—bring them a cup of coffee or a glass of water. Take a minute during prayer time and say a prayer for someone else. If you're in recovery, volunteer to do a practical task, like cleaning up after the meeting. If we can't change the world, at least we can do our part to keep it going.

✑ Day 6 ✑

"Thank you for letting me be of service." Although people who attend Twelve Step meetings often say that, we don't have to be in recovery to say those words.

Gratitude Focus: We can be grateful for all the opportunities we have each day to serve.

ༀ Day 7 ༁

Give freely of what you've been given. Give freely of what you hope to receive.

Just give. Service is its own reward.

Prayer: *Show me how best to serve. Teach me to balance service with taking responsibility for myself. Help me remember that service is an important part of finding my place in the world, bonding with others, and taking care of myself.*

Goals, Hopes, and Dreams

✎ Day 1 ✎

Passion waning? Bored? How long has it been since you set new goals? How long has it been since you checked in with your heart so you could remember your hopes and dreams?

I first learned about the value of goals when I began recovering from codependency. Until then, I hadn't thought much about formalized goal-setting. My first informal goal was to get as far away from the raging fire of addiction as I could. I had other vague dreams. I wanted work that was meaningful. I wanted a family, a husband, kids.

These goals and dreams weren't conscious. But a pattern had already begun to emerge. Whenever I said what I wanted, that event would come to pass—as long as what I said I wanted concerned my destiny. The timing wasn't mine. I always had to wait. And the reality of experiencing what I wanted was always different from the way I imagined it would feel. Reality was more of a struggle than the utopia I pictured in my dreams. And getting what I wanted never made me happy unless I was already happy first.

I have wanted many things in my life. When I was younger, I wanted to be a good wife, a writer, and a counselor. Later, I wanted to be a good single parent and earn enough money to support my kids. Accomplishing all these things required me to learn about myself.

When I had matured, I wanted other things. After my son, Shane, died, I wanted the pain to stop. But one day, I realized that the absence of pain would mean I hadn't loved Shane as much as I did. This is when I became willing to learn about healing my heart and grief. I wanted to get up again and experience new things. I wanted to jump out of airplanes. I wanted to see the world: Egypt, Israel, China, and Tibet. I wanted to help other people whose hearts were broken through the loss of a loved one.

What do you want to do? There must be something that motivates and interests you. There's magic in setting goals and saying what you want. "Be careful what you ask for, you might get it," people warn. "Nothing comes to a dreamer but a dream," other practical people advise. Well, when dreams come true—even if it's just for a moment— that's all right by me.

And the difference between our fantasies—how we think something is going to play out—and the way they actually do? That's the stuff lessons are made of. It's called life. Experience as much of it as you can.

Value: This week we'll explore the value of goals, hopes, and dreams.

༄ **Day 2** ༄

He carried a wish list in his wallet. It included everything he'd like to get, experience, do. He made it, then put it away and forgot about it. "One by one, all my wishes came true," he said. "Maybe it's time to come up with some new goals."

Application: *It may be time to wish and dream for a little while—if you can't remember the last time you thought about your goals, if all your dreams have come to pass, or if all your dreams have faded.*

ᘓ **Day 3** ᘒ

"I want a new home, a great job, and lots of money," one man said.

"What practical steps are you taking to help that happen?" I asked.

"I'm not very good at practical steps," he said. "But I'm an expert at dreams."

It's important to fantasize, but if you want your fantasies to materialize, you have to take practical steps. Turn dreams into achievable written goals.

It takes courage to go for what we want. Giving something our all, then failing, is a risk. Anyone I know who has accomplished anything of value has failed on the road to success.

Challenge: *The hardest thing about going for our goals, hopes, and dreams can be fighting off that part of us that says, "What's the use?" Ordinary people can accomplish extraordinary things when they make a choice to do something, then surrender to God's Will.*

ᘓ **Day 4** ᘒ

We all have to grind through life at times. Sometimes life's events dictate and shape our course, but enduring is a survival skill. Don't make it a way of life.

Inventory Focus: *Are you doing the big and little things* *in life that are important to you? Do you create land mines on your path instead of setting new goals?*

∽ Day 5 ∾

"I've known intellectually that the journey is as important as the destination," one man said. "I've finally made *enjoying the journey to achieving my goals* one of my goals too."

Action: *Infuse your life with passion. Inject new goals. Make a list. Update it frequently. What are your goals, dreams, hopes, and wishes? Divide your life into these six areas: spirituality, money, love (family, friends, and romance), work, personal (health, appearance, etc.) and fun and adventure. Can you try to write down something for each?*

Reached your goals and dreams? You're already successful at what you do, and now you're bored? Set a new goal. Help ten people accomplish the success you've accomplished. See what kind of zest that adds to your life.

Bored with work, a hobby, or even your recovery group? Maybe you need a change, but maybe the change doesn't mean throwing away something that's perfectly good. Set some new growth goals. Challenge yourself.

Not sure what you want? Explore it. Go see. Learning about what you want and don't want is an important part of life too.

Combine passion with service, and watch where your goals take you.

ༀ **Day 6** ༁

Wishes, hopes, and dreams are all around us. Catch just one of them. Write it down on paper. Let it become real.

Gratitude Focus: I can be grateful for all the dreams that have found me. Dreams can be a way for God to reveal his plans for me.

ༀ **Day 7** ༁

This is how it usually works. I realize I want something. Then I want it so badly it drives me crazy. But I can't have it. I'm finally forced into letting go, surrendering to God's Will, taking the next step and doing the next thing, even though it's not what I want. Somewhere along the line, my efforts start to transform into what I said I wanted.

Setting goals is magical. So is God's Will.

Prayer: Show me which dreams to pursue. Teach me the value of what I want and what you want for me.

Stepping into the Unknown

✎ Day 1 ✎

I ran into a friend at a restaurant one day. I asked her how she was doing.

"My divorce is final. I'm newly sober. My alimony has run out. And I realize I don't have a clue about what I want or what's next in my life."

"Isn't that great?" I said. "You're in the Unknown."

She scowled at me. I smiled. When it's not us, we can see all the possibilities and potential from entering that vast domain of not knowing what's coming next. We know clearly that it is a necessary place to be. If we knew what was coming next, it would be limited by what we have experienced so far.

When change is happening to others, we can sit back and be philosophical. We can remind our friends and loved ones that *not knowing* puts us on high alert. It makes us more aware and sensitive. We're open to learning, seeing, and experiencing new things. Sometimes having our lives turned upside down is essential because the process allows us to be transformed. Hanging on to what is familiar wouldn't work. We know all of this because we've been there many times. We know that there's nothing to fear, because before long, a new life will appear.

We know all this until the Unknown happens to us.

I met my daughter for lunch at a restaurant. She asked how I was doing.

"I'm scared," I said. "I've had a pretty clear path for the last few years. I've known what was coming and what to expect. I'm just finishing up the last pieces of everything I know to do. After that, I don't have a clue."

"Isn't that great?" she asked. "You're entering the Unknown. How exciting for you."

It was my turn to scowl now. There are times we feel comfortable and secure in the daily routine of our lives, relationships, and work. Other times, this sense of security becomes shaken and dislodged. We become acutely aware of how vulnerable we are, and that while there may be answers to our problems and a path for us, we don't have that information yet.

I have seen strong women cry and get shaky knees. I have heard brave men admit to feeling a wave of fear and wishing they had their mothers. We stand at the edge. For a moment in time, what we see looks dark. We don't know whether monstrosities loom or whether everything will be fine. People tell us we are guided and to trust in a benevolent plan, but we know that anything can happen.

Take a deep breath. Feel your fear. Then carefully take one step at a time.

Value: Whether it's an attitude of wonder and awe that we cultivate or a place that we've chosen or has been forced on us, letting go of what's comfortable and familiar and stepping into the Unknown is the value this week.

ᴄ Day 2 ᴄ

"I just ended a five-year relationship. I'm changing jobs. And my youngest daughter is moving out of the home," a woman said to me. "I'm normally a strong, brave woman. But my knees are shaking. My palms are sweaty. I cry for no reason at all. Why am I facing fear now?"

Application: Entering the Unknown happens at important junctures in our lives. It can happen when we get sober or begin recovery for something else. It can happen when we get married, get divorced, or end a career. It can happen later in life, when our children grow up and leave home. Sometimes we see it coming. Other times it happens suddenly and quickly. We're starting over again, and we don't know what to think or expect.

Other cultures honor and revere that mysterious place called the Unknown. Native American culture and Buddhism teach people to beware and be aware of it, because facing the Unknown is a powerful time when forces are working hard to help us create the new.

ᴄ Day 3 ᴄ

Sometimes, in the way that life has of bringing times of change, we may be doing a lot of letting go of people, places, and things all at once. It's the end of something, but nothing new has begun. It may be hard to know what to do next. We try to do the next thing, but nothing feels right. We may keep reaching out for a person or dream, expecting it to be there.

If you love something, let it go? If it comes back to you, it's yours? Say whatever you want about letting go.

The truth is, letting go can hurt.

> **Challenge:** *The hardest thing about letting go is coming to grips with the idea that the person or dream is gone. Be gentle with yourself. Don't expect too much. It's hard to keep up with reality when it changes all at once.*

ᵛᵗᵃ Day 4 ᴧᵛ

Isn't it funny how we can sense change coming, yet turn a blind eye to all the signs of change?

> **Inventory Focus:** *Can you be gentle and understanding —patient with yourself and life—when you go through a time of change?*

ᵛᵗᵃ Day 5 ᴧᵛ

"When I go into the Unknown, I immediately start making lists," one man said.

We each respond differently to loss, letting go, and the Unknown. We may try to fill up the vacuum immediately with something else. That usually doesn't work, at least not well.

Try to be as present as you can for what you're going through.

> **Action:** *Protect yourself. You're vulnerable now. Do the simple, easy things that need to be done, one task at a time, even if nothing feels completely right. Remember the basics of self-care. Eat. Sleep. Shower. Get plenty of rest. Talk to trusted friends. Express what you're feeling at the moment the best that you can.*
>
> *We may vacillate between anger, rage, guilt, and sadness when we're letting go. And then we may go*

numb and not be able to think clearly. Don't worry about that; your ability to think clearly will return. Don't do anything that hurts yourself or anyone else. That won't help. It'll make things worse. Lists may help us stay on track.

Try not to see the big picture right now. It probably hasn't been shown to you yet.

∽ Day 6 ∼

The thing with transformation is that when we least expect it, a new life appears before our eyes.

Gratitude Focus: *It is tough to be grateful for anything when we let go. If nothing else, we can try to be grateful for the kind people in our lives.*

∽ Day 7 ∼

We may feel alone. We're not. We may feel unsupported and unguided. We're not. The angels are holding us each step of the way.

Prayer: *Hold me close when my heart hurts and when I feel alone and afraid. Help me be kind to others and myself.*

Duty

ᵥᵥ **Day 1** ᵥᵥ

I was talking to a friend about something I didn't want to do but believed I needed to do anyway. I was dreading it and feeling irritable. Often when we talk like that, other people scowl and say, "Oh don't let *shoulds* control your life. If you don't want to be doing it, don't."

But this man understood.

"At the risk of sounding old-fashioned," he said, "duty calls."

What's there to say about duty? It's a job, for different reasons, that needs to be done—whether we really want to or feel like it.

"I haven't watched a football game from beginning to end without interruption for almost three years," a father of two young children said. "I adore and love my children. But sometimes I miss football too."

One of the children began rubbing his eyes. "Ready for your bottle?" the father asked. The child nodded. The man turned away from the football game on TV, patted his son on the head, and went to the kitchen to fix the bottle instead.

I learned about duty when my children, Nichole and Shane, were born. A lot of things needed to be done to take good care of them, whether I felt like doing all of those things or not.

I learned throughout the years that even the most exciting jobs have uninteresting and sometimes distasteful duties. When I worked for a daily newspaper, I loved my job. I enjoyed covering front-page news. But many of the stories I was assigned to were duty stories.

Sometimes a relative needs help. A parent may get sick, grow old, or become vulnerable or infirm. While we don't want to become duty-bound and strap our entire lives with *shoulds,* there are times in any relationship—family, romantic, or friend—when a code of honor rules and we do what we must.

"I believe we have deeper duties too," a friend said. "If we've been given sobriety, spiritual growth, or gifts, I believe that it's our duty to pass those gifts along and share them when we're asked."

It may be something we need to do to maintain a relationship with someone we love. It could be something we need to do that we'd rather not as part of taking care of ourselves. The task may be something we need to do for work or as part of our spiritual mission in life.

Go ahead. Say *arrrgh.* Dread what you're about to do. I know, there are more interesting and exciting things calling your name. But for a moment, can you put those things aside?

Value: The value we'll look at this week is putting one foot in front of the other and doing what we must when duty calls.

ᴇᴠ **Day 2** ᴀᴠ

Of course you're feeling grumpy. You're about to do something you'd rather not do. But once you get done feeling irritable, could you try to be a little lighthearted about it? Maybe there will be a pleasant surprise when you do that task you dread doing.

If nothing else, think about how good you will feel when it's done.

Application: *We may dislike some of our personal duties, but ignoring them will only leave us feeling worse. Often these duties are part of a larger goal that we desire, such as spiritual growth, a good credit rating, a healthy relationship, or a new job. But usually duty runs even deeper than that. Responding to the call of duty is essential for self-worth.*

ᴇᴠ **Day 3** ᴀᴠ

Many of us get confused about recognizing our true duties. Some of us may think our duty is to respond to every request. That's not responding to duty. It's a co-dependent response to life.

Then we may sway the other way. I'm only going to do the things I want to do. "Nothing more and nothing less," we think. On some other planet that might work, but it doesn't work well here.

It's hard to do things we'd rather not do, especially once we get in touch with ourselves and have some sense of what we like and what we don't like. Once we show up, however, it can be challenging to respond to our duties with poise, an open heart, and grace.

Challenge: *The hardest thing about duty is deciding what our duty is. The voice of true duty is distinct. Learn to recognize it when it beckons.*

✎ Day 4 ✎

Responding to duty separates the men from the boys and the women from the girls. Can you let go of what you would rather be doing and do something else?

Inventory Focus: *Have you ever ignored or neglected your duties? What were the consequences of that? After my divorce, I was swamped by bills and not making much money. I hid those bills deep in a drawer. That didn't help. I could still hear them calling my name from any room in the house. Is some duty whispering—or screaming—at you right now? Wouldn't it be easier to just say yes?*

✎ Day 5 ✎

Sometimes when I have particularly dreadful duties to perform, I literally make myself sick. I might get in an accident or start feeling feverish. "If I really get sick," I think, "then I'm home free. I don't have to do my duty, and I've got a good excuse."

That's not the way it works. If it's a true duty, I end up doing it anyway—with a fever, the flu, or a bandage on my leg.

Action: *When it's time to do something you must, it helps to find something to like about the task, or a good reason to do it even when you don't want to. It helps to find something to be passionate about, even when it's a* little thing like what you're going to wear. Getting clear on why you're doing it can be helpful too. "I don't want to do this, but I feel it's important to do because . . ." Feel all your feelings, and then get to work. You've got a job to do that needs to be done. Usually the worst part about fulfilling your duties is the dread you experience first.

ᵕᐡ **Day 6** ᐡᵕ

Thank God for grace.

Gratitude Focus: *We can be grateful when we sense God's role in our duties.*

ᵕᐡ **Day 7** ᐡᵕ

Once we begin chipping away at our duties, a new feeling begins. Even when we don't want to be doing what we must, we may find ourselves almost enjoying ourselves. We begin seeing the gifts and feeling the reasons for why we're doing what we are. We may feel stronger, closer to God, closer to other people. At least we feel good about ourselves.

Ignoring our duties piles up guilt and anxiety. Fulfilling true duties energizes us. It feels good in the end.

Prayer: *God, help me do the hard stuff that I need to do. Help me do it with an attitude of service and love.*

Boundaries

✺ Day 1 ✺

"My son had been out of my home for years," a friend told me. "He wanted his independence but didn't want to pay the price. He always needed money for food and rent. Each month, I told him this was the last time. He'd either be grateful for my help, angry that I was upset, or both. 'Other parents help their children,' he'd say. 'You're the only parent I know who's so cheap.'

"It was a battle. Each month I lost," this friend said. "It took a lot of getting angry, giving in, and feeling used before I could say no and then stand behind what I said."

If a stranger demanded that we do something we didn't want to do, we'd probably refuse. It's harder when that person is someone we love.

Sometimes giving is a good thing. Other times it's not. It can be hard to recognize when a pattern of being kind turns into a pattern that's sabotaging both the other person and us. Each time an incident happens, we think, "Oh, this is just happening once. And this is the last time." Until it happens again.

I first learned about boundaries when I loved an alcoholic. I kept thinking that rescuing that person would help him and benefit us. I wondered what would happen if I withdrew my help. Would the relationship end? Would that person die? It was hard for me to see that not saying no to him was hurting him, our relationship, and me.

Boundaries aren't a value to be applied only in situations with alcoholism. It can be easy to get lost in what other people want in many situations—both healthy and dysfunctional—in work, recreation, and love.

Saying no to someone else and saying yes to ourselves is an important part of love.

Value: Whether we call them boundaries or limits, recognizing them is the value this week.

ᘛ Day 2 ᘚ

"I don't think of myself as codependent," a friend said. "I call myself an *overcarer* instead. The problem is, when I care too much about one person, someone else doesn't get enough of my attention."

The person we're neglecting by giving too much is frequently ourselves.

Application: We have a buzzer that goes off when we're doing something we don't want to do that's truly not our duty, when we're being manipulated, or when we're not being true to ourselves. Whenever we think we hear that buzzer making noise, it probably is (and has been for a while).

ᘛ Day 3 ᘚ

Boundaries aren't limited to saying no. Boundaries reflect what we believe we deserve. Some people were born into situations that encouraged listening to and trusting themselves. Others had their right to self-respect violated at an early age. If our ability to trust ourselves was tampered with when we were young, we may have to work extra hard to acquire and keep boundaries—and self-esteem—in place.

"Someone who barely knew me mentioned to a friend that he thought I was selfish," a woman said. "For the next six months, I had the worst time setting limits. I kept trying to prove how unselfish I was."

No matter how many boundaries we've set, it's not unusual to still feel guilty each time we say no. We may be afraid that we'll lose the other person, or that he or she will go away if we say no. But when we don't honor ourselves by setting boundaries, we're the ones who disappear.

Challenge: The hardest thing about boundaries can be recognizing that we've lost or misplaced ourselves again. Maybe we could look at setting boundaries as an ongoing process of discovering who we are.

✤ Day 4 ✤

The boundary question isn't "Can I keep doing this?" It's "Do I want to?"

Inventory Focus: Some have a high tolerance for pain. It takes a lot before you recognize that a situation hurts. How has it worked out for you when you've neglected yourself or overcared about someone else? Are you open to discovering and saying what's right for you wherever you are? Just because something was right for us yesterday doesn't mean it works today.

ᴄᴧ **Day 5** ᴧᴜ

A situation happens. Then it happens again. At first, we may react mindlessly or try to do what we think is right. After a while, we get angry and feel used. That buzzer is saying, "Something's wrong."

After struggling through confusion, fear, sadness, and guilt, we finally set a boundary. We may look back on the situation later and wonder why it was so hard. After all, that choice—to respect ourselves—was the best thing we could have done, for everyone involved.

Telling people no doesn't just respect ourselves. It respects other people too. It tells them we believe they have some capacity to take responsibility for themselves. Setting a boundary can often be more helpful than the overcaring we've done.

> *Action: Sometimes a situation is an opportunity to give or to learn something new. Other times it's an opportunity to say no. Be considerate of other people. But instead of responding mindlessly, take a moment. Ask yourself what you want. Are you doing it because you've made a decision to do it? Or are you feeling pressured by someone else or by inappropriate guilt? Before you can tell other people what your limits are, you have to tell yourself.*
>
> *If it's a confusing situation where children, mental illness, or addictions are involved, talk to knowledgeable people. Figure out what reasonable boundaries are in that situation.*
>
> *Once you have decided on a boundary, inform the other person. Be as clear, nondefensive, and nonattacking*

as you can. Once in a while, you may need to get firm or raise your voice. Usually you can be respectful toward others when you say no.

When you say the hard stuff, for just a minute, you might have to close your heart. If someone is manipulating you or is addicted—or if you love that person a lot—being open may weaken your boundaries. Your boundaries are liable to collapse.

You know it's important to tell children no. And remember the grown-ups you say no to are often just big kids. Sometimes they keep doing things to us just because they can. Remember, you don't set boundaries to control other people; you set them to respect yourself. Once you set a boundary, enforcing it is up to you. You may have to get creative, depending on the circumstance and how much power you have.

❧ **Day 6** ☙

The more we believe that we have a right to our wants and needs, the more gently we can say, "This is what's right for me."

Gratitude Focus: *We can be grateful for situations that challenge us to set boundaries because they push us to find self-esteem.*

❧ **Day 7** ☙

I used to wish they sold boxes of boundaries at convenience stores. Now my thinking has changed. I wish they sold big boxes of learning to trust ourselves.

Prayer: *Please show me which boundaries to set and when. Guide me through those complicated situations when setting boundaries hurts.*

Wait and See

ᴄᴠ Day 1 ᴬᴺᵛ

He asked her for a date. She agreed. "I thought he was funny and cute," she said. They went to a restaurant. She watched him slam one drink after another, change moods, and ignore her. She watched herself start to freeze.

"I can't believe this is happening," she thought. "I can't believe I'm mixed up with an alcoholic again." She went into the bathroom, said a quick prayer, and then went back to the table.

"I don't mean to hurt your feelings," she said. "But this evening isn't working for me. I'm going to call a taxi and leave."

She called a friend later that night. "I knew he drank," she said, "but I thought he drank socially. I decided to give him the benefit of the doubt. I have a real thing about not getting involved with alcoholics. I can't stand being around it. How could I not see this?" she asked. "How could I be so dumb?"

"I don't think you were stupid at all," her friend said. "You made a decision to wait and see. You waited, you saw, you left. That's what dating is about. It's a chance to wait and see whether someone is the person you want."

No matter how hard we might try to see a situation clearly, sometimes we can't. It might be a situation at work, in a friendship, in love. It might concern a lesson we're in the midst of learning. Whether we know it or not, we're muddling about in the dark.

Denial is a powerful force. It can protect and buffer us from shocks too intense to absorb. Or we can be in the dark about something and not be in denial. There may be aspects of a current or future event that are concealed from us. There's no way we could know what reality is yet because we haven't been shown.

Clarity is a value, but it's also a gift. It arrives in its own time. *Wait and see* combines the value of patience with the gift of seeing clearly.

Value: *This week we'll look at how smart it can be to wait for the lights to come on.*

✌ Day 2 ✌

Is this marriage going to work? What is the other person going to do? What's really going on? What do I want to do?

If you jump to conclusions, you will be hopping all over the place. Instead of relieving anxiety by making decisions when you are unclear, reduce anxiety by deciding to wait and see.

Application: *Whenever you are saying, "I've got to know right now," it's a good time to wait for clarity. Sometimes life slams on the brakes. It makes us wait and tries to show us whatever we're not seeing now.*

༙ Day 3 ༙

I've got to have him. Can't live without him. It must be love.

Whoa. Just a minute. It's only the second date. For many of us, learning to wait and see is a value that's been hard-won.

Some of us thought waiting to see meant waiting to see whether the other person would choose us. Or we jumped in and then waited for the other person to be who we wanted him or her to be.

Once we see clearly, that person we were convinced we had to have may not even be someone we want. Life may be trying to point out something better than anything we could have chosen ourselves.

Challenge: It's hard to calm down and live with the anxiety and uncertainty of saying, "I don't know" when the unsolved mystery involves someone we love or something we want. Sometimes that mystery is minor, but the anxiety can make it feel big. Other times what we're waiting to see affects our entire life course. Saying we're going to wait and see can mean acknowledging the possibility of a loss.

Wait and see is more than a decision. It's an act of faith.

༙ Day 4 ༙

I banged my head on a metal ledge. The pain was fierce. Two days later, I finally went to see a doctor. "You've got a concussion," he said. "One of the problems with a concussion is that you're stunned. The concussion keeps you from seeing clearly enough to know that you're hurt and need help."

That wasn't the first time denial had been one of the symptoms of a problem I had. When I was using alcohol and other drugs, I left a trail of destruction in my path like a wake behind a boat. But each insane thing I did made perfect sense to me. When I was trying to make an alcoholic behave, I could see that he kept drinking and things weren't improving. But a symptom of codependency was a fog that kept me from seeing that I was hurt and needed help.

We can become enmeshed in many situations where we're aware that something is wrong, but we don't know what it is. Whenever I hear myself saying, "This can't be happening," it usually is.

Inventory Focus: *Instead of berating yourself for not knowing something you don't or can't see, are you willing to be gentle with yourself while you wait for clarity?*

ᏯᏯ Day 5 ᏯᏯ

"I didn't know whether my son was an alcoholic or whether he was doing normal experimentation," a woman said. "I talked to people. I worried about when or whether I should put him in treatment. But the day it became time to do that, I just knew. It became perfectly clear."

"I'm in a relationship right now, and I'm not sure where it will go," another woman said. "Sometimes the hardest thing in the world is to not obsess and just let it be what it is."

Wait and see doesn't mean we completely let go. It means that for a while, we decide to hang on loose.

Action: Can you remember a time when you let go and patiently waited for clarity to arrive? Instead of trying to force things, can you wait until that feeling of rightness comes around again? Relax. Let the picture come into focus instead of staring at it so hard.

༒ Day 6 ༒

"More shall be revealed," a friend said, quoting the Big Book of Alcoholics Anonymous.

"And if you knew what was going to happen," another friend said, "you'd just try to control that too."

Gratitude Focus: We can be thankful that we don't have to see the whole picture—only what we're shown today. And no matter what the situation looks like now, there's always more to come. Confusion and not knowing can prepare us to see something new.

༒ Day 7 ༒

Oh, I see. There really is a plan.

Prayer: Help me let go of urgency and fear. Teach me to be confident that things will work out, even when I don't know how it will happen.

Be Not Afraid

༼ Day 1 ༽

My daughter, Nichole, was reading her son a bedtime story about fear. She told him that sometimes he'd be afraid of dangerous things, like putting his hand on a hot stove. Other times, he'd be scared of nothing at all. See! There's really not a monster under the bed. He can tell people when he feels afraid and ask them to stay with him until he feels safe. Or he can hold a favorite toy until he feels okay.

"I wish it was that simple," I said to her later. "What about those times we feel afraid and a monster is really there?"

Nichole knew what I meant. I was with her at the hospital when her second son was born. When he had trouble breathing and they whisked him to ICU, she looked at me. "Tell me everything is going to be okay," she insisted. I couldn't speak. I averted her eyes. My fear was making her fear worse. I had to leave the room and pray. Thank God, Nichole's husband is a rock. He went into the ICU and stayed until his newborn son began breathing on his own.

Usually our fears are fantasies we've created in our mind. But once in a while, we find ourselves living through and facing our worst fears. And sometimes when we're really afraid, we have to draw on the strength of someone who is not as scared as we are.

It can be tempting to dwell on difficult times from the past, in order to give credibility to the *what ifs* that disrupt our peace. But we can also think about how much we've survived and how well we've done, in order to remind ourselves how brave we are.

Be not afraid. That doesn't mean don't feel fear. From anxiety to panic to terror, all the shades of fear need to be acknowledged. Our emotions, however, are not who we are.

Value: This week we'll look at fear, along with the values of bravery, courage, and peace.

ᴄᴡᴀ Day 2 ᴀᴡᴄ

"Make a list of your fears," a man said to his friend.

"I can't," his friend said. "I'm too afraid to look."

Application: Sometimes fear warns us of impending danger, like when we're about to get hit by a car. Other times it startles us, like when we hear a loud noise. Or it makes our heart race and our breath go away during an anxiety attack. Or it dwells beneath the surface, making us cold, restrained, controlling, or mean. Sometimes what we don't know is what scares us. Other times our past experiences create terror. We dwell on possibilities and create fear in our mind. Fear usually feels cold and makes us tense. As soon as we recognize that fear is there, it's time to look at it so we can find our way back to peace.

☙ Day 3 ❧

There are many kinds of fear. For example, when fear warns us of danger, we heed the warning, and thank fear for being our friend. On the other hand, fears that we're not conscious of can be a problem. We may not know we're afraid, but our actions are motivated by fear.

Some people can't just feel the fear and let it go, as experts suggest. We feel it, but the letting go part doesn't work. The fear goes on and on. We're facing our fear, but we're not winning. The fear dominates us.

Some people who struggle with chronic anxiety need to seek professional help, which can be a valid step toward peace. And remember what C. S. Lewis said: "Grief can feel like fear."

It can be challenging to determine which fears we need to face.

Challenge: *Fear feeds on itself. It can convince us that fear-based actions are the appropriate course. But the hardest thing about fear isn't fear. It's taking the time and effort to restore ourselves to peace and then knowing when to be brave.*

☙ Day 4 ❧

I was driving to a situation that could be ugly. I called a friend. "Please talk to me," I said. "I'm having an anxiety attack. I can hardly breathe."

"I didn't know you had anxiety attacks," she said.

"Sure I do," I said. "Doesn't everyone feel afraid?"

Inventory Focus: *What is the bravest thing you've ever done? Remember, bravery isn't the absence of fear.*

Bravery is when you act even though you feel afraid. Maybe you could be a little more tolerant of others and yourself. Instead of proclaiming, "No fear," you can be vulnerable enough to tell yourself and someone else what frightens you.

ᴗᴖ Day 5 ᴖᴗ

"How do you face fear?" a woman asked.

"I suggest doing one thing each week that scares you," I said, even though Eleanor Roosevelt said to do one thing each *day* that scares you.

Action: Make a list of your fears, known and unknown. Then tell yourself, someone else, and your Higher Power what's on the list. This idea is borrowed from the Twelve Steps of Alcoholics Anonymous. Next make a list of ten things, like deep breathing or praying, that help you feel peaceful, or at least help you make peace with the fear. Learn to recognize fear. Then figure out what you need to do to make yourself feel safe.

We each have similar—and different—things on our list of fears. Sometimes our fears are deep rooted. They got stuck in us from our past. We each have different ideas and levels of actions we're ready to take to be brave and face fear. For some, it might be riding in an elevator. For others, it might be expressing how they feel.

It's important to know your limit. But sometimes it helps to push yourself a little when your fears limit you too much.

﹏ **Day 6** ﹏

I've traveled alone to Pakistan, Algeria, and East Los Angeles, and I was perfectly safe. Yet, in my own home, I've given myself a concussion, burned myself, and fallen down the stairs.

There are certain things we need to do to responsibly protect ourselves. I recently asked a friend to pray for my safety on a potentially hazardous journey. She said, "I'll ask. But know that God is already with you."

Wherever we go, God's there. Make yourself safe wherever you are.

Gratitude Focus: *Instead of resisting our fears or feeling ashamed of them, let's try reverse psychology and be grateful each time one comes up.*

﹏ **Day 7** ﹏

During a crisis, we need to remember that when we step up to the plate, with God's grace, we will prevail.

Prayer: *Help me take reasonable steps to protect myself. Then would you please do the rest?*

Colors

ᘉᕽ **Day 1** ᕽᘉ

Imagine a world in black and white, maybe gray. Boring, isn't it? But some of us want our emotional lives to be like that.

A friend told me about a song he played in the car while driving with co-workers. It was a song about the richness of life—the high points (marriage, the birth of children) and the low points (death and loss) and how good it all was.

"One of the guys in the car wondered how you could possibly consider loss good," my friend said. "I tried to explain, but I'm not sure he got it."

I understood. All our experiences are rich colors that make a full life.

Have you ever cried so hard that you thought you would never stop? Have you ever laughed so hard you cried? Have you ever known someone you didn't want to live without—a friend, lover, or relative? Have you ever been so forlorn you thought you'd never be happy again? And just when you were about to lose hope—or right after you did—your Higher Power came through? Have you ever felt so angry while driving that when a street-light went out, you thought your anger did it? Have you ever felt so angry you wanted to break something, stomp, or spit? Have you ever wanted something so badly—like sobriety—and been so afraid you couldn't have it you were willing to go to any lengths to achieve success?

It's important to feel all our emotions—jealousy, desire, anger, love, despair, and the taboo feelings. I know, feelings can be a pain in the neck. Feelings can make us feel ill. If we don't feel them, they don't go away. And it can take awhile to figure out what to do with them after we notice they're there.

Red with anger. Green with envy. Blue with sadness. The pink cloud of recovery. Go ahead. Pick a color.

Value: *Please don't settle for only black and white. Vibrant, colorful emotional health is the value this week.*

⌘ Day 2 ⌘

I'm a dinosaur. I still believe in—and love to talk about—feelings. But like someone said, "Dinosaurs are 'in' right now." They're the rage.

Application: *When we get stuck in a feeling such as depression, anger, or guilt, when we feel ashamed about what we feel, or worse yet, when we go numb, it's time to reconnect with our emotional world. What's really going on under the numbness, irritation, or guilt? It's okay to talk about it. Feeling our emotions doesn't mean walking around exploding. We can open up our heart and share some of the tender feelings—the ones that make us vulnerable—with someone we love.*

❧ Day 3 ❧

"I'm trying to deal with my feelings the best that I can," a woman said. "I don't force them on anybody or hold anyone responsible for what I feel. I try to be aware of what I'm feeling, feel it, and then release the emotion. Let it go. Sometimes I know what I'm feeling, but sometimes I don't. A whole bunch of emotions get stuck together and come out in a bunch."

"What you're doing sounds right to me," I said. "And meltdowns are good."

As hard as we may try to ignore what we're feeling, sometimes the force of our emotions is more than we can control. The anger, sadness, frustration, hopelessness, and fear that we've been trying to wish away spill out all at once.

"My husband is really good about his meltdowns," one woman said. "He has one every other week or so. If I go in the room with him, he'll spill emotions on me. But if I leave him alone, at least he won't follow me around dripping his meltdown on me."

A frustrating event can trigger a meltdown. Sometimes it's minor or unrelated to what we've been feeling—or trying not to feel. Everything we've been working so hard to not express comes out. It's like we're a ripe blueberry, plump with emotions, that explodes when it gets poked.

See how much better we feel after we've melted down?

Challenge: The most difficult thing about feeling emotions can be connecting with them. It can feel much safer to live in our head. Surprise! The feelings we tried so hard to ignore were exactly what we needed to feel to get our lives on track.

ᴠᴧ **Day 4** ᴧᴠ

What's your favorite feeling? Least favorite? How do you deal with anger? What feelings are taboo for you? Have you ever gotten even with anybody and punished him or her when they hurt your feelings? When was the last time you melted down? Maybe instead of punishing people when we feel hurt, we could take a risk and tell them how we feel instead?

Inventory Focus: *Are you willing to expand your emotional world?*

ᴠᴧ **Day 5** ᴧᴠ

Please don't let our world—or your world—turn black and white. I know it's tough grinding through emotions. I spent years crying every day after my son died. I hated it. But eventually I began to see the gift: at least I had loved so deeply and intensely that it broke my heart.

Action: *These are things that help me get in touch with feelings: emotionally honest people, writing in my journal, good movies, good books. Exercising, especially yoga, helps me get unstuck. Acupuncture helps, too, when automatic pilot has set in. If you really get stuck, you may need professional help. Anger management classes and therapy are options too.*

I believe the world will assist you with whatever you need. The right person or incident will come along to trigger you, poke you, help you feel. You might work hard to not feel, at first. But life is persistent. Some of those disruptive incidents are gifts to help you come back to life.

⋙ Day 6 ⋘

Remember that there is a difference between feeling angry and turning resentful. And after we feel angry or hurt, it's time to practice forgiveness. There's a difference between feeling jealous and harboring ill will. But if we don't get all those feelings out first, we won't be able to get values like forgiveness and goodwill to work.

Gratitude Focus: *We can be grateful for each feeling that comes our way, even the ones we don't think we should have.*

⋙ Day 7 ⋘

Did I forget to mention that joy is a feeling too? But the trick is, when we look for joy, it's hard to find. Joy is made up of all the other colors that exist. Joy is when we're willing to surrender to all our experiences and all our emotions.

Prayer: *Help me to be not so frightened of feeling my emotions. Send me exactly what I need to stay emotionally alive.*

Forgiveness

ᔕᕀ Day 1 ᔕᕀ

Did you ever do something stupid that hurt someone's feelings? Did you ever treat someone wrong and there was no justification for how you behaved? I have. It's an awful place to be, when we realize what we've done.

The more we value that person, the more we want them to know how genuinely sorry we are. We'd give anything to see their facial muscles soften and hear them say, "It's okay."

I first learned about the value of forgiveness when I was in treatment for chemical dependency. I didn't realize how much I'd hurt other people until I'd been sober for a while. When I became aware of my guilt, it was paralyzing and thick. I just wanted it to go away, and I didn't think it ever would. The antidote for guilt is forgiveness. Asking for forgiveness from others or God puts us in a vulnerable place. There is nothing we can do except wait until we get word—and believe—that it's okay.

I recently read a magazine article about the physiological benefits of saying, "I'm sorry." Acknowledging to someone that we've hurt them, saying we're sorry, and genuinely meaning it improves health.

Recovery programs have known for a long time that

becoming aware of the harm we've done and making direct amends are essential for the well-being of the person making amends. But making amends doesn't just benefit us. It helps the other person too.

As hard as I try not to, I still make mistakes and do things that hurt others. Sometimes I know what I'm doing is wrong, and I do it anyway. Other times it's an accident.

Forgiveness isn't just a value we need if and when we're recovering. It's a value we'll need all our lives.

Value: Forgiveness has many components: self-inspection, self-responsibility, compassion, living by a set of ethics, letting go of our defenses, letting go of resentments and judgments, humbling ourselves, wanting to be close to God, acknowledging to other people that they're important to us, knowing that others care enough about us. All these aspects of forgiveness are good. Whether we're extending or receiving forgiveness, it's the value this week.

✔ Day 2 ✔

We will sabotage ourselves if we don't believe we deserve success. Maybe we could try a different approach? Stop torturing ourselves for the things we have done wrong, then try forgiveness instead. We can make amends by doing service work—a way of keeping that self-sabotaging guilt at bay.

Application: Sometimes people don't know how to directly ask for forgiveness, but their behaviors will tell us that's what they're saying. Whenever somebody asks for forgiveness, whenever we have a list of resentments, whenever we've done something wrong, it's a good time to start making things right.

ᔦ Day 3 ᔧ

We can get ourselves in a knot about guilt. We tell ourselves the other person deserved it, we had our reasons, or our circumstances were *special*. Or we convince ourselves that if we admit we did wrong, we'll have less self-esteem than we do—and we don't have that much right now.

There are situations where someone keeps doing the same thing over and over to us. Before they've finished saying sorry, they're doing it again. In these circumstances, it may be time to see whether an addiction is involved or whether boundaries need to be set.

Then there's artificial guilt, the kind we need to reject. We get it when others are trying to manipulate us, when we say no, or when we take care of ourselves.

Guilt can be part of grief. The guilt isn't real, but it feels real because we think we should have or could have done something to prevent the loss.

We may feel like we need to hang on to our resentments because if we don't, we'll be vulnerable again.

Sometimes people aren't ready to forgive us yet, or we're not ready to forgive them. It can be difficult to forgive when someone hurts us a lot. Forgiveness can take a long time.

And if we don't feel our feelings first, forgiveness won't stick.

Challenge: The most challenging thing about forgiveness isn't believing God forgives us. It's learning to forgive and making peace with ourselves. If you can't do it all at once, try baby steps. See how good it feels to let love in?

ᘒ **Day 4** ᘓ

He yelled at his friend in front of a group of people. Later he knew he had to make amends. "Should I apologize to everyone that was there or just the guy I yelled at?" he asked his wife.

"Well, if you make your amends to the guy as loudly as you yelled, you don't have to worry. Everyone will hear you," she said.

> *Inventory Focus: Need to say sorry to someone or let someone off the hook? You can't do anything about whether other people forgive you. And sometimes you can't just whisk away your guilt. But you can start repairing relationships and self-esteem by taking steps to clean up your side of the street. Even if the other person did something to you, you still have a side of the street. Does it need to be swept?*

ᘒ **Day 5** ᘓ

Forgiveness is like certain foods. We need to develop a taste for it. Once we do, we're hooked.

> *Action: If you are doing something that is creating guilt, stop doing it as soon as you can. Figure out reasonable, sane ways to make amends. Sometimes it means changing your behaviors and saying sorry. If saying sorry will cause harm to someone else, you may need to eat that guilt. Don't say sorry when it will make the situation worse.*
>
> *If you need forgiveness, ask. Religious rituals may help. And Steps Four through Ten of Twelve Step programs work if you do what the Steps suggest.*

If someone asks you for forgiveness, seriously think about saying yes. Even if they don't ask, do you really want that resentment eating at you? If you've done your work and still feel guilty, remember that guilt comes in waves. Acknowledge the feeling, and then go on with your life.

Forgiveness is humbling and may be the hardest work you'll ever do. It's worth the effort. It tastes good.

～ Day 6 ～

If we can't forgive someone else or ourselves, compassion is the next best thing.

Gratitude Focus: *Don't just say, "There but for the grace of God go I." We can be thankful for all the times it was us, when we received enough grace and forgiveness to get through it or change.*

～ Day 7 ～

Want to be a true environmentalist? Go ahead. Improve your own health or someone else's. Say sorry when you've hurt someone. And forgive them when they say it to you.

Prayer: *Help me understand the value of each human being, including my own value. Teach me when and how to forgive.*

Goodwill

ᴄᴏ Day 1 ᴀᴏ

Have you ever envied someone else's good fortune? Consider the friend who calls with a different ring to her voice. Instead of sharing her troubles and woes, she proceeds to tell you good news. Something exciting, financially beneficial, glamorous, wonderful beyond belief has happened in her life. It's not a fantasy. It's one of those rare moments when a dream has come true.

"That's wonderful," you may say, meaning every word. At first.

"Why her?" You may later think. "What about me? When am I going to get a break?" As hard as we may try not to feel that way, a little jealousy, envy, and self-pity replace the joy we felt for our friend.

Most of us want other people to be successful and happy. We really do. That's not the problem. The problem comes when we think they're going to be happier or better than we are.

I first learned about the value of goodwill after I got sober. The first couple years, I thought my financial struggles were appropriate. I was paying my dues to rebuild a life. After all, success takes time. But my financial struggles went on and on, while I watched my friends buy new cars, new clothes, and beautiful homes. I didn't have a car or even a phone at times. I began to get concerned.

On one particularly poverty-stricken Christmas, a friend stopped by with gifts for my children. That year, those were the only gifts they had. I was grateful she stopped by. But I felt a wisp of envy. Why couldn't I have enough money to buy presents for my family?

"She doesn't have anything that belongs to you," I reminded myself. "She has what's come to her as a result of what she's done and the individual circumstances of God's Will in her life. So do I."

Sometimes we know when we're envying and resenting others. Other times it's a subtle undercurrent that we're not aware of, but it invades our lives. It may only be a slight feeling of smugness when we hear that something unfortunate has happened to someone we perceive as being more fortunate than we are.

> **Value:** *Goodwill isn't just the name of a secondhand store or a phrase used in songs during the holiday season. It's a particularly challenging value to practice, and it's the one we'll look at this week.*

༺ Day 2 ༻

So an acquaintance is younger, is prettier, is in better shape, has a nicer home, has a more luxurious car, is more successful, has fewer problems, leads a more interesting life. Maybe this person is more creative, more popular, more gifted, more talented, more skilled. Or maybe we don't see this person as *more* than we are. Maybe we regard this person as a jerk, but for some reason, no one else, including God, sees this—because this person appears to get all the breaks.

Ill will can take many shapes and forms, from feeling disgusted with other people to feeling satisfied when they have problems. Sometimes ill will takes the form of coveting what others have. Goodwill, on the other hand, has only one shape and form. We wish other people well, we hope God blesses them abundantly, and we want them to be as happy as they can be.

Most of us understand the fundamentals of goodwill, but it's tempting to slip. We may find ourselves doling out small portions of goodwill. We recall past slights and ask, "Don't you know what a jerk this person is?" Practicing this value is difficult.

> **Application:** *Whenever we find ourselves wishing other people didn't have what they do, maliciously gossiping, judging, thinking dark and bitter thoughts, or thinking if others had less we'd have more—whenever we start subtly or overtly giving other people the evil eye—it's time to stop cursing them and practice goodwill instead.*

～ Day 3 ～

Looking at other people with jealousy, envy, and mean and bitter thoughts isn't new to our world. The concept of giving other people the evil eye has been around for a long time. It's mentioned in almost every religion and culture in the world.

Sometimes we're not conscious of the darker thoughts we think. We might believe that ill will and the feelings connected with it—envy, jealousy, resentment—are wrong. So when we feel that way, we push those feelings and thoughts aside.

"I remember lying in bed one night, tortured by my marriage, but believing it would violate my religious beliefs to get divorced," a woman said. "I started counting the years until I thought my husband might die. A light came on. I realized that wishing him dead was a lot worse than saying good-bye."

We want to believe there's a balancing force that prevails in the world. And while this force is balancing things out, we'd like to get some of the good stuff too. Hey, God, remember me?

> **Challenge:** *The hardest thing about practicing goodwill is believing that when we're happy for other people— even when they're happier than we are—it will make us the happiest people in the world.*

✺ Day 4 ✺

"What comes around goes around" is a phrase most of us have heard. Instead of waiting until other people get the pain and suffering we believe they deserve, how about generating goodwill so that can come around to us?

> **Inventory Focus:** *What's the thing you're most jealous or envious of in others? What do you find yourself judging most? What's your sore spot, the place you feel you got cheated out of something important in your life? Sometimes I wonder why other people get to have their children and I don't have my son, Shane. Maybe what you really want is to fill the empty spot and the hole in your own life.*

✎ **Day 5** ✐

Some people suggest that thoughts are prayers. Maybe we could make sure what we're praying for is good.

Action: Feel all your feelings. Repressing thoughts of jealousy, envy, or bitterness doesn't help. It makes you dishonest and passive-aggressive. Perhaps you are pretending to like someone, but you think they're a jerk. As soon as possible after identifying your feelings, begin practicing goodwill. Force it, fake it if you must. Deliberately think positive thoughts toward whomever you just wished ill.

✎ **Day 6** ✐

Thank God we're not in charge of karma. On second thought, maybe we are—our own.

Gratitude Focus: We can be grateful whenever something good happens to someone else.

✎ **Day 7** ✐

"Want what people have" is a saying from Alcoholics Anonymous. It doesn't mean covet their belongings. It means let other people's success inspire us to live by values that will help us be successful too.

Prayer: Help me believe that blessings will be given to others and myself. Protect me from the ill will of others. Help me be a force for good.

Harmony

ᡣᡯᡣ **Day 1** ᡯᡳᡢ

Did you ever go to a concert? The musicians all play the same song, but each one has a different part in creating the music. Whether they're creating somber minor chords or cheerful major chords, the band is working together in harmony.

I had a difficult time with harmony when I first became introduced to it. It was right on the heels of beginning my codependency recovery. I became exposed to groups of people I had never encountered before. Some I found interesting, some irritating. I thought owning my power meant crashing like a cymbal wherever I went. It took a while to learn that I could own my power more effectively by harmonizing than by being a discordant note.

Harmony isn't just a value to apply in our relationships with other people. We all go through changes in our lives. At one point, we may be going through a time of discipline, keeping our nose to the grindstone. Then it may be time to play. Then we may move into a time where we have a lot of emotions to deal with, and we're moving slowly. Other times we're sailing through in high gear. Instead of expecting situations to change, we can learn to harmonize with them.

We don't go to a funeral in a party mode, and we don't wear our workout clothes to our office job. We harmonize our actions with the environment we're in. We don't have to live in conflict with ourselves, others, the events in our lives, or even with the different hats we wear.

If we really aren't compatible with certain situations, it may be time to leave. But a lot of the time we can make sweet or at least interesting music by harmonizing—or by being flexible enough to meet the situation halfway.

Harmonizing is more than just a musical phrase. It's more than live and let live. It's living together. It's compatibility, being on the same page. It involves enough self-awareness to be ourselves, and enough adaptability and flexibility to fit that self into different situations. Harmonizing means opening up, listening, letting go of self-will, practicing nonresistance, and extending tolerance.

Value: Harmony is the value this week.

ᘓᘏ Day 2 ᖰᘁ

Do you harmonize with other people or do you expect them to harmonize with you? When someone says no or something you don't like, do you find yourself sucked into an argument and ready to disagree? What would happen if you said, "Okay"?

Application: Whenever we find ourselves in discord with other people, the circumstances in our lives, or even what we want, need, and feel, it may be time to stop forcing things and harmonize a little.

ᑐᑓ **Day 3** ᑐᑓ

"We're on the same page" is a popular phrase. It means that people are working together or have similar intentions or goals in a relationship. If nothing else, it can simply mean that people are in agreement about a plan for an hour, day, or week.

It can be tempting to prove how different we are from the people around us. We can be different. It's sometimes important *not* to compromise. But other times, by harmonizing our intentions with those around us, we're able to make that difference count.

Sometimes it's fun to say or do things to deliberately challenge or provoke others. Conflict can be good. And sometimes it's important to stand up for our rights.

But some of us get addicted to chaos. We like the drama that comes from uproar. We may begin to mistake the high-adrenalin emotions created by chaos for love or think that's the way life always needs to be.

We don't want to get in a rut. But don't underrate compatibility. It's okay when things go smoothly too. Don't worry. Change and challenge will come along soon enough, on their own.

> **Challenge:** *The hardest thing about harmonizing can be overcoming the fear that we'll lose our identity or that we're somehow giving in and losing by harmonizing with someone—or something—else. We can be ourselves and still be part of a couple, team, environment, or group. And we'll have a lot more energy when we're not using it to overpower someone or resist.*

ᴖᴖ **Day 4** ᴖᴖ

Have you ever felt like you were forcing your way through life? Have you ever made a decision, and even as you were making it, something inside you was already tensing up and saying, "That's not right"? Heaven knows I have times when I can't stop myself from crashing about. We can go through difficult situations with a lot less effort when we harmonize with ourselves and God's Will.

> *Inventory Focus: Your head says, "Work harder." Your heart says, "Rest." Your head says, "I've got to have a relationship right now." Your heart says, "I need time to be alone." Have you ever said yes and meant no? Are you willing to live in harmony with other people and yourself?*

ᴖᴖ **Day 5** ᴖᴖ

It feels different at the ocean than it does at a bowling alley. At the ocean, you take off your shoes, let the wind blow on your face, listen to the sound of the surf. When you go to the bowling alley, you put on your bowling shoes and get ready to roll. You're not a different person in either of these situations. You're the same you, but you're harmonizing with the environment you're in.

Most of us don't go to the beach to bowl. But we may walk into many situations in our lives with that same out-of-tune attitude. Just because something is different from what we're used to doesn't mean that it's wrong.

> *Action: The next time you find yourself in conflict with someone, instead of arguing or trying to prove they're wrong, try harmony instead. Just for a moment, try to see*

the situation from someone else's point of view. If there are parts you agree with, say that. At least acknowledge how interesting it is that they see things that way. Don't just be tolerant. That can be condescending. Be respectful. Now you're in harmony. Go ahead and share what you think and feel too.

Kahlil Gibran wrote about how you need to bend a little. Then you won't break.

✺ Day 6 ✺

What a boring world it would be if everyone and everything were exactly the same. On the other hand, we have more in common with every living being than we think. Harmony helps us discover what our common grounds really are.

Gratitude Focus: *We can be grateful for those situations, groups, and events in our lives that challenge us to learn how to harmonize. They can teach us more about who we are. And if we stay open, we might learn something new.*

✺ Day 7 ✺

Sometimes it's fun to sing a solo in the car or in the shower. But harmonizing makes beautiful music too. Even conflicts can be brought into harmony with God's plan.

Shhh. Can't you hear it? It's the music and rhythm of life.

Prayer: *Teach me that by harmonizing, I tap into your power.*

Letting Someone Help

໑ **Day 1** ໑

I was walking up a steep mountain in China. I was tired. Steps loomed endlessly ahead of me. Just when I thought I couldn't go one step farther, a group of women climbers came along. They noticed my weariness. One stood in front of me, another behind me, and one woman grabbed my left hand. When I couldn't take one more step, their support and energy carried me along. We walked together for a while, until I felt strong again.

Later, I found it remarkable that I allowed myself to receive other people's help.

Knowing we can take care of ourselves is good. But we can take that too far. It's easy for most of us to give to other people. It puts us in control. We're more vulnerable when we let someone take our hand and lead the way.

Help and support are all around us, no matter what our needs are. The help may come in the kindness of strangers. It may take the form of a group, such as Alcoholics Anonymous, Al-Anon, or The Compassionate Friends (a group for people who are grieving the death of a loved one). It may be a friend who reaches out to help us, or a relative, or someone at work.

The assistance offered may be practical: advice, money,

teaching us a skill, making us a meal when we're sick. The help offered may be emotional support, someone to listen and care. Sometimes just having someone present is what we need.

I like knowing other people are there for me. But I have had a fiercely independent, stubborn streak since I was a child. Some of it began when I was ill, couldn't attend school for a year, and had to stay home all alone and teach myself my studies because my mom worked a lot. I can still be like a two-year-old trying to tie my own shoes. "Just leave me alone, I can do this myself"— whether I can or not.

It's still hard for me to let other people help. I'm afraid I'll be indebted, that there will be some kind of trick or hitch, that I'll lose my pride or lose control.

It's good to have boundaries about whom we let help us and what kind of help we receive. But c'mon. Some of us have carried this illusion too far; we struggle on, thinking we are all alone and have to do everything ourselves.

Value: Asking for and allowing ourselves to receive help is the value this week.

✑ **Day 2** ✑

Giving and being of service to others bonds us to them. When we accept help from others, it allows them to feel close to us.

Application: When we're trying to do it by ourselves and it's not working well, when we know we're in over our head and we're about to drown, when we're doing it by ourselves but it's difficult and hard, or when some-one gently offers, it may be time to say, "Help." Don't forget to say, "Please." Be a little vulnerable. Relax those defenses. Let yourself receive.

✌ **Day 3** ✍

"Just call if you need help," people offered when I was having surgery on my knee and finger. "Okay, I will," I said. I knew that even though I'd be on crutches and have a cast on my arm, I'd do everything humanly possible to get through my recuperation alone.

My first night home from the hospital, I had to lower myself to the floor and drag myself across the room when I needed anything—like a glass of water. It was hard to drag myself back to the couch with one arm in a cast and hold anything in the other hand. I needed the free hand to push myself along. I figured out a system. I could first move my water in the direction I was headed. Then after I put it down, I could use that hand to get leverage to move myself. Quite a picture, isn't it?

One of my fears is that I'll be needy and dependent, expecting other people to take care of me as if they were substitute parents, like I did in my codependent years. There are times when we can do it ourselves. But wouldn't a little help be nice?

Challenge: *The hardest thing for me about asking for and receiving help is that I don't want to be a burden to anyone. What's the hardest thing for you? Maybe we could trust other people a little.*

✌ **Day 4** ✍

Don't just let others help you because you think it will benefit them. Receive help because it helps you.

Inventory Focus: *Watch your reaction when people offer help. How do you feel? What do you think? What's your verbal response? What do you do when you need help and no one offers assistance? Do you ask? You're really not as alone as you think. You have a Higher Power. And sometimes God uses people to respond to your requests.*

ᘓ Day 5 ᘔ

She was newly sober, forty-eight hours away from her last drink. She was in a restaurant with a group of people more seasoned in recovery. "It's odd," she said. "I feel a power to stay sober when I'm with this group that I don't feel when I'm alone." It can save our lives to recognize that some things *can't* be done on our own.

Action: *In ancient times, people who were masters used to make newcomers prove how much they wanted help. They had to sacrifice and show by their actions that they were sincere. Many treatment centers used to make drug addicts and alcoholics prove that getting help wasn't a whim or temporary fix. The purpose of asking for help isn't just to let the other person know you need it. When you ask, you recognize how much you need help—and then you're open to receive.*

ᘓ Day 6 ᘔ

Thank God for every person who's been there to help you. Then thank the people too.

Gratitude Focus: *We can be grateful each time we need help, and then allow ourselves to receive. It's one more step to shattering that illusion that we're in this thing alone.*

✒ **Day 7** ✒

An acquaintance is one of the most brilliant doctors I know. It's almost miraculous, the way he works.

"I'm responsible for what I do, and I feel good about my work," he said. "But I humbly recognize that it's not me. It's a Higher Power thing."

Prayer: *Open me up so I can receive help from other people and so you can work through me too. Help me learn that I don't have to do it alone, no matter how alone I feel. Show me that even if I can do it myself, sometimes I can do it better with help.*

God's Will

✎ Day 1 ✎

How do we know what God's Will is, especially when we're running around with a severe case of self-will run riot? How can we make sure the choices we're making are God's Will when our options seem confusing and we're not sure what to do? What about when we do something we think is God's Will and it doesn't work out? Do we blame ourselves? Or do we count our mistakes as lessons we needed to learn along the way?

Sometimes when I recover from a particularly exhausting bout of self-will, I think that my *mistakes* were just a waste of my time. But then something happens, and I see that my worst mistakes are recyclable. What I learn from mistakes translates into something else that works out for the good.

We do have choices, and they have consequences. Most philosophers agree that free will is the greatest gift given to human beings. And we're responsible for what we choose—or don't choose. But most of us who have some practice with God's Will agree that there's a little extra something taking place.

Getting a publishing contract to write my book *Codependent No More* was a passion and a dream I'd had for years. But when I went down into my basement to write it, I hit the wall. I didn't know what to say.

It finally turned into one of those surrender deals. "What am I thinking of?" I said to myself. "If it's God's Will, the book will get done. And if it's not part of God's plan for my life, then it doesn't matter whether it gets done or not. There's something else I'm meant to do." I could see how futile and ridiculous it was to worry about whether anything would—or wouldn't—work out.

No matter what happened or didn't, God's Will was more than enough.

Since that time, I've had many occasions when I've either forgotten that lesson, or when my self-seeking has gotten in the way. And I seriously questioned that lesson when my son died. Although I've still got a few questions and comments about that whole ordeal, I've basically made my peace.

With all my ups and downs, I still believe with all my heart that God's Will is the best thing around.

Value: There's a peace, a harmony, a rhythm to God's Will. It's a solid undercurrent, a path that takes us through, over, or around whatever we face, including the Unknown. We don't always know when we've gotten out of or away from it, but we can sure feel it when we get back on track. God's Will is the value this week.

∽ Day 2 ∾

God's Will. It's safe. A worry-free place. Pretty magical too. Why is it so hard to keep surrendering to it when self-will is so dreadful and so much work?

Application: It's time to remember how easy and suffi-cient God's Will is whenever we get crazed about what's going to happen. We'll get all the power we need to do everything that needs to be done. And every single thing that is supposed to take place will, in its time.

✒ Day 3 ✒

"What are these people talking about?" I wondered when I first heard people talk about surrendering to God's Will. The Big Book of Alcoholics Anonymous calls it living in the fourth dimension of existence. It made no sense to me at all.

Sometimes when we try to intellectualize it, the idea of God's Will looks a little bizarre. Or we look around at the world and wonder whether God's Will still works.

What's more irritating than someone blaming every choice they've made on God? "Yes, I did that," they say, "but God told me to. It was God's Will." Or how about when someone tries to impose his or her will on us by calling it God's plan? There's an old joke in the publishing industry about the writer who submits a manuscript and says, "God told me to send this to you and that you'd publish it." And the publisher writes back and says, "That's not what God told me."

God's Will isn't something we can do in our head. Figuring it out will make us nuts. It's a feeling we get that all is well, even if it's not what we want.

Challenge: The biggest problem with God's Will is us.

∽ Day 4 ∾

She had a problem that went on for years. She kept trying to trust, but there were times it was hard. The days it was difficult, her voice was tense, strained, and I could tell she'd been crying. Finally one day, the entire problem got resolved.

"Isn't God's Will great?" she said. "At least in the end?"

Inventory Focus: *Have you had any experiences trusting God's Will and seeing how that worked out? Maybe you could draw from those experiences to help you endure any current difficulties? Often God's Will means doing the quiet, ordinary things. I don't know why, but it seems that frequently we need to focus on surrendering to God's Will at the eleventh hour.*

∽ Day 5 ∾

Recovery programs suggest that if we surrender to God's Will, "clean house," and make our amends, we'll become more aligned with God's Will. We'll be given the right thought, word, or action. We'll be shown what to do next, and when.

Action: *"Sought through prayer and meditation to improve our conscious contact with God,* as we understood Him, *praying only for knowledge of His will for us and the power to carry that out." This is the Eleventh Step of Alcoholics Anonymous. Seems pretty clear to me. Just do it the best that you can.*

∽ Day 6 ∾

Thank God for all the loving, kind, beneficial things done in the name of God's Will.

Gratitude Focus: *We can be grateful that no matter how confused we get, whenever we truly seek God's Will for us in any situation, there it is.*

∽ **Day 7** ∾

What makes us think that anything we could conceive could be better than what God has planned?

Prayer: *Help me stop wearing myself out with all the drama and quietly trust that your Will is taking place. Show me that in any situation, if I ask what to do, I will be shown.*

Faith

Day 1

It's silly and a little embarrassing. I call it the *feather principle.* It means two things to me, but the closest word I can find to describe it is faith. Whenever I see a feather lying on the ground—and sometimes one will even blow into the house—it's a reminder to me that I'm where I need to be right now and that everything is going as planned.

I think I originally got the feather idea from a movie I watched a long time ago. Whenever something distressing happened to the main character, Forrest Gump, a feather would float through the air. It's one of those things that stuck with me. It's a symbol that I can calm down and trust where I am.

I was discussing spirituality and faith with a friend. "It takes faith to believe in tomorrow. But I think it takes more faith to believe that I am where I'm meant to be in my life right now," he said.

It's easy to have hopes and dreams for our future, to have plans. We all need those. They help direct our path. And having things to look forward to, even the little things, makes life fun.

But having faith that on some far-off day our lives are

going to be great and better—believing in tomorrow—doesn't take nearly as much spiritual discipline as it does to believe in today.

Sometimes I really don't like some of the things I have to do or that are going on in my life. I tend to weigh myself down with mumbling and grumbling, balking, digging my heels in, obsessing, dreading, wondering whether I can trust God, and generally making things worse than they are. It's not enough that I have to go through, endure, or do what I must. I make the job three times as hard with my attitude.

Feathers float. When I see one, it reminds me to lighten up. Believing in destiny and floating through it are what feathers mean to me.

Value: Faith is the value this week.

∽ Day 2 ∼

I don't know why I get so worked up when I have to travel somewhere. It's almost like I convince myself I have to flap my arms like a bird to fly the plane. We can make things harder than they are. But sometimes all we need to do is show up.

Application: Whenever we feel like we just can't do what needs to be done because it's too hard, we can look around. We're right where we need to be at this moment. Instead of being so heavy, we can let the wind blow us to where we're going next.

∽ Day 3 ∼

I first learned about having faith for today in my early

years of sobriety. My life felt uncomfortably odd. Even though I was doing what people told me to do—taking responsible care of myself—it felt like something was wrong. I heard about a good therapist. He lived far away. I didn't have a car, but I was determined to go see him. I thought he could tell me what I needed to do to make my life better and right.

I made my appointment and eagerly waited for that day to arrive. "My life will be better then," I thought. "It won't be like it is now." The day arrived. I got on a bus, transferred, got on another bus, transferred, then rode another bus to his office. Then I sat down and told him everything that was wrong.

He listened patiently, then leaned back. "I'm about to hear the missing piece that will change my life," I thought.

"Sounds to me like you're right where you need to be," he said.

The missing piece was faith.

Sometimes when things aren't working, it's a warning that we're heading in the wrong direction. But we can still believe in today and where we are now. It's the only way to get wherever we're going next.

Challenge: *It's easy to tell other people and ourselves what we're doing wrong. It's easy to give advice. If you'd just do this or that or these other things, then your life would be right. Yes, we need to work on issues, solve problems, try new approaches. And sometimes we need information about how to do things, including living our lives, that we don't have now. But it doesn't take much faith to criticize other people or ourselves. It takes a lot more faith to look at others and ourselves and believe* *that we are doing the best that we can—and that what we're doing is good enough.*

∽ **Day 4** ∾

"I saw the craziest thing when I was running," a friend said. "A man was on a skateboard. He had a big dog on a leash next to him. He had attached a big stick to the dog's collar—just inches away from the dog's reach. The dog kept running faster and faster to get the stick, not knowing it was attached to his head. It was a trick to pull the man along. I hope the dog didn't figure out what was going on," he said. "If he did, he probably bit the man."

"Yes, but tomorrow I'll be more fulfilled." Yeah, and the dog will get the stick.

Inventory Focus: *Are all your goals, hopes, dreams, wishes, and plans for tomorrow? Maybe you could look around and see the beauty of where you are now.*

∽ **Day 5** ∾

Some of the experiences we go through are hard. We get heavy at times.

"I'm drowning in my grief," I told a friend after my son died. "It feels like I'm swimming across an ocean, and I'm getting tired."

When it's too difficult to keep swimming, float.

Action: *What's more irritating than someone condescendingly telling you to smile when you feel glum? Feel all your feelings. Don't let anyone tell you they're wrong.*

"I reached in my pocket today and found joy, happiness, success, and gratitude," a friend said one day

when he called. At first I didn't know what he was talking about. Then I remembered. Awhile back, when he was going through a difficult time, I had given him four little stones, each one painted with one of those words.

It's important to believe in tomorrow. But give yourself the gift that keeps on giving. Believe in today.

∽ Day 6 ∼

Sometimes the greatest act of faith we can perform is to stop worrying, obsessing, or grumbling—just for the moment. Then take a break and do something nice for ourselves.

Gratitude Focus: *Let's find one thing to be genuinely grateful for about ourselves.*

∽ Day 7 ∼

Longing for tomorrow? Nostalgic for yesterday, when times were better? Tomorrow's "good old days" are happening right now.

Prayer: *Help me remember that everything happens for a reason. And even if I don't know what that reason is, you do.*

Weathering the Storms

ᏙᎵ Day 1 ᏃᏙ

I was driving to an errand one day when a storm suddenly dumped water out of the sky. I couldn't see out the car windows. The streets flooded. I had to pull my car to the side of the road. I was scared. I sat there and prayed for more than an hour. Finally, I noticed the sun peeking through the clouds.

Metaphorical storms hit our lives as well. Our job may be threatened. Financial emergencies may arise. Our car may break down. A run of personal happiness may be interrupted by an attack of self-contempt or despair.

Sometimes the storms feel personal. If a friend betrays us, lies to us, or manipulates us, we feel attacked. But it may be that our friend is in a downward spiral and getting hit by a different storm—his or her behaviors don't have that much to do with us.

A situation at work can feel personal, especially when it jeopardizes our income or job. But the shift may have to do with management, corporate budgets, or something that has little to do with us. We didn't cause it, and whatever is happening is not a consequence of what we did.

The storm has as little to do with us as does a hailstorm that appears in the sky. Everything happens for a reason. But the reason for some of these storms may have nothing to do with us.

When personal storms occur, it's time to pull our car to the side of the road and figure out what we need to do to protect ourselves. In the middle of these storms, we don't necessarily need to understand the lesson we should be learning. Rather, we need to calmly give ourselves over to a survival mode and commit to weathering the storm.

Value: Developing confidence in our ability to weather storms is the value this week.

～ Day 2 ～

I was in a small village in China when the rain came pouring down. I opened my backpack, dug around, and fished out exactly what I needed. Fleece jacket, raincoat, weatherproof pants. "Go ahead," I thought, "let it storm."

Application: Whenever a storm hits, it's time to dig into our backpack of survival skills. I know, we thought those days of surviving were done and we were on our way to being happy, joyous, and free. We are. But every once in a while, a storm comes along. Let's use those skills we learned.

～ Day 3 ～

Guilt is part of grief. Often when a storm comes up, it involves a loss. It may be the loss of security, a friendship, or a job. When losses occur, we may immediately think, "I had this coming because of the things I've done. I deserve this." Then we go over all the things we still feel guilty about. Worse yet, we then fail to take proactive steps to improve whatever problem we're faced with.

We wouldn't stand outside and let it hail on us, thinking we caused the storm or it was punishment for something we've done. Or maybe we would?

Storms are challenging enough to survive. Don't make them worse by torturing yourself. Unless you're getting fired from your job for not showing up for work (in which case it's a consequence created by your actions), you don't deserve it as punishment.

Some people sit and watch The Weather Channel hoping for a storm system to appear. We can get so bored or so used to fighting storms, that we hope one comes along to divert us from our lives. It can be challenging to determine which storms we're creating, and which ones we're not.

Challenge: The hardest thing about weathering storms can be that many of us don't know how to protect ourselves. It's okay to put on our rain gear. And sometimes it's good to come in out of the rain.

ᥲᑫ Day 4 ᒷᥣ

Look at all you've overcome and gotten through so far. What makes you think you can't get through this?

Inventory Focus: Stop panicking. Calm down. You're good at responding to what others need. Are you willing to quietly figure out what you need to do to protect yourself? Try thinking of this as an adventure, a chance to prove to yourself how much you've learned.

ༀ **Day 5** ༅

"I started crying one day. It was just a small thing that triggered it. Someone said something," a woman reflected. "The problem was, once I started crying, I couldn't stop. I didn't understand what was going on. There was no apparent reason for why I felt so sad. For days, all the things in my life that had been working seemed to stop."

Little storms of despair, hopelessness, or self-hatred may squall up out of nowhere in our lives. We can hunker down and protect ourselves even when the storm is inside us.

> **Action:** *Don't back yourself into a corner. What are your options? Don't just come up with Plan A. Figure out a Plan B too. It might not be time to do anything yet. The storm may only be threatening. But see how much better you feel when you know you can make some choices.*
>
> *Sometimes you've got to make emergency decisions. Instead of standing there saying, "I can't believe it's raining," remember first things first. If someone who is usually trustworthy hits you with a manipulation, don't stand there trying to get him or her back on track. If an idea occurs to you about what to do to take care of yourself, don't instantly reject it, thinking, "Oh that's silly and I don't need to do that."*
>
> *The first thing to do may be to protect yourself.*

ༀ **Day 6** ༅

Thank God when the rain stops and the sun shines again.

> **Gratitude Focus:** *We can be grateful we'll be guided through everything in our lives, including how to survive storms.*

ᴄᴧ **Day 7** ᴧᴜ

Floods, hurricanes, wind gales, blizzards. Sometimes our personal problems seem to rival the intensity of these forces of nature. Most of us have been through everything short of tsunamis. Don't stand there trying to control these storms. Rather, let each storm wear itself out.

Prayer: *Teach me to respect the power of storms. Help me remember that this, too, shall pass.*

Self-Acceptance

ᢗᠬᢇ **Day 1** ᢒᠬᠣ

Self-acceptance is a more humble term than *self-esteem* or *self-love*. Self-love has tones of narcissism—me first and to heck with you. Self-esteem rings of pride—holding ourselves up higher than everybody else. Self-acceptance is that gentle place we get to when we make peace with who we are.

"For a long time, when I talked to certain people, I got squeamish and uncomfortable, like it wasn't okay to be me," a friend said. "I thought it was me being uncomfortable with myself. I've finally learned that I'm responding to how uncomfortable some people feel about themselves."

We might feel so awkward about ourselves that we believe we have to be different from who we are. Some of that comes from low self-worth, not believing that we're okay. Or it can stem from a need to control. We think if we pretend to be different or better, we can manipulate how other people feel about us.

Some of us don't know who we are. Other people tell us to be who we are, but when we look in the mirror, we see a blank spot. If we weren't encouraged as children to be who we are—or if we were forced to be something or someone other than who we are—it can take time and effort to gain a comfortable sense of ourselves.

Yes, we have things to change and learn. And throughout this year, we are working on values to apply. But whether we're at work, in relationships, or trudging our spiritual path, we don't have to be anyone other than ourselves. We do our job, we love other people, we correct our mistakes and try to change. But not from that awkward, uncomfortable place of faking who we are.

Value: *Self-acceptance is the value this week.*

༺ **Day 2** ༻

I was telling a friend about some cherry cough drops. "They're so tasty that I eat them like candy," I said. "I eat a whole box in a sitting."

"I know a lot of people who have quirks, but who have no idea that what they do is strange," he said. "You're conscious of the things you do that are odd."

What a gift when we can make peace with God, our family, our past, or someone we've been estranged from for years. What a gift when we can finally make peace with ourselves.

Application: *It is time to apply some self-acceptance whenever we find ourselves trying to impress others, wondering whether we're good enough, or trying too hard to say the right thing. It's fun to keep up with the latest trends, but self-acceptance is always in style.*

༺ **Day 3** ༻

When we're going through times of change and transformation, we can get confused. We knew who we were, but we don't know who we're becoming.

We can buy into being socially or politically correct. We think if we want to fit in with the crowd, we can't be ourselves. It hurts when others reject or judge us. It hurts more when we reject ourselves. Or we can go the other way and randomly rebel.

Sometimes self-acceptance hurts. Not liking our behaviors is important for change. But it's hard to change what we do until we accept first that we're doing it.

It's not difficult to be who we are. That comes naturally. The challenge comes when we think we should be something else.

Challenge: Pay attention to your self-talk. Beware of put-downs like "Why are you feeling that way?" "Can't you do better than that?" "If people really knew you, they wouldn't give you the time of day."

The biggest challenge to accepting ourselves isn't what other people tell us. It's the things we tell ourselves.

✧ Day 4 ✧

"I want you to meet these people," I told a friend. "I think you'll like them and I think they'll be helpful in your career."

"Great," my friend said. "Can I just be myself or do I have to be someone else?"

Inventory Focus: Are there any areas in your life where you feel that it's not okay to be who you are? Who are the people in your life who trigger a lack of acceptance of yourself? Do you feel like it's okay to be who you are when you talk to God? What's the hardest thing for you to accept about yourself?

It's easy to look around and think people are better than you are. (Sometimes it's easy to think, "They're all nuts.") I used to categorize people in two ways: them and me. But now I have learned that it's just one big us.

∽ **Day 5** ∼

"I'm really cranky," a friend said. "When I'm at work lately, I've just got to bite my tongue or put my hand over my mouth."

Accepting ourselves doesn't mean we do or say whatever we want. Sometimes it means letting ourselves have our bad days without imposing them on anyone else.

Action: *It's good to have people who challenge you to improve. But what a relief when you find people who totally allow you to be who you are. If you haven't received acceptance from others, maybe you could take a minute and give some to yourself.*

You only need to accept who, what, and where you are today. Then the oddest thing happens. You're either given the power to change, by your Higher Power, or given the grace to live with the rest.

∽ **Day 6** ∼

"I'm grateful for my recovery groups," a woman said. "Hearing the little things that people say about who they are and how they feel helps me believe that I'm okay too."

Gratitude Focus: *Thank God for validation. If we open our heart and really listen to others, validation is usually around us.*

〜 Day 7 〜

We have so much in common. We're each different too. Our dark emotions, the tender ones, our needs, desires, and hopes. The way we laugh, the things we find funny, the way we express ourselves, the shape of our body, the way we let other people know we care. Our struggles, mistakes, conflicts—even our battles with ourselves. Those odd little things we do like eating a whole box of cough drops because we think it tastes better than candy.

Can you remember a time, before life got to you, that you innocently accepted who you are? Maybe you could recapture some of that feeling. Bring who you are to the world.

Prayer: *Help me make peace with myself.*

Paying Dues

ᓑᓑ Day 1 ᓑᓑ

Did you ever get a punch card from a coffee shop? If you buy nine coffees, you get the tenth free. Even though you're not paying for it, you know this purchase isn't free. The price was factored into earlier purchases. But still, getting something free is sweet. We feel like we deserve what's handed to us.

Have you ever had the experience of moving into an apartment or house, and even though it looked okay, the decorating wasn't yours? "I've got to do something to make this mine," you think, even if it's just painting a wall.

Many things in life are like that. They don't feel like ours—and we don't feel like we deserve them—until we put time and effort into them. Then we feel like they belong to us.

In Alcoholics Anonymous, there are no dues or fees. The only requirement for membership is a desire to stay sober. But we do certain things. We work the Steps. We go to meetings. We work with other alcoholics. And although our sobriety is a gift from God, we begin to feel like we deserve sobriety by working to make it ours.

Paying dues applied in my career as a writer. Struggling for the first seven years, making almost nothing for the work I did, wasn't just something I had to do to acquire new skills. By putting that effort into my career, I felt like I made it *mine*. And I know we can't own or possess a person, but the giving we do for our children—or for other relationships—isn't just for the other person. Giving bonds them to us.

Most of us like the concept of getting something for free. But little in life can compare to feeling like we deserve what we've earned.

Value: Whether it's building a relationship or investing in our sobriety or our career, paying dues cheerfully is the value this week.

﹏ Day 2 ﹏

Sometimes I think we create land mines in our path until we've paid enough agonizing dues to justify forgiving ourselves.

Application: When it's time to pay dues, we can find a way to embrace the task at hand and really own it as our own.

﹏ Day 3 ﹏

Desiring instant gratification can sabotage our efforts at paying dues and working toward specific goals. We want what we want, when we want it, which is usually *now.*

Other people tell us if we want a relationship, just go after it. If we want a certain career, all we need to do is go to college and get a degree. If we have a dream, all we have to do is set a goal. They leave out the paying-dues part.

When we find ourselves being tried and tested, we

may think the obstacle is a sign that we're heading the wrong way. Sometimes it is. Other times an obstacle is challenging us to invest more of ourselves so we can genuinely own the endeavor.

We may have spent years investing energy in a bottomless pit. We were giving to someone who had no intention of giving back. We may have decided not to give that much of ourselves again. The problem with paying dues may be deciding which people and projects deserve our attention and efforts.

Challenge: *The biggest challenge to paying dues is that we may think we're exempt. We think things should be easy. But if things come too easy or cheap, we may not realize how valuable they are.*

༄ **Day 4** ༄

A friend trained hard for an athletic competition. His team took third place. After the main competition, he was invited to be on a spontaneous, last-minute team. This last-minute team took first place in another event.

"Getting first place was fun," he said. "But it was a fluke. We worked much harder for third place, and I deserved that medal."

Inventory Focus: *Are you being asked to pay dues in some area of your life—recovery, a relationship, a career? When I first got sober, I had problems with my driver's license. I knew I had abused the privilege of driving. I took a bus for years and didn't even look into getting my driver's license back. Finally, I looked up at the heavens. "Enough's enough," I said to God. "Can I please* *get my license again?" When I called the motor vehicle department, I learned that I could have been driving years earlier. The law said my driving privileges could be restored, but I didn't believe I deserved that privilege. Is there some area of your life where you could look at the tally sheet and discover your dues are paid in full?*

⇜ Day 5 ⇝

"My sister asked me what I wanted at a time when I was floundering," a man said. "I told her and she responded, 'Well, then you better change what you're doing because you're not behaving like that's what you want.'"

Are you willing to pay the price for what you say you want?

Action: I know, you've given before and sometimes haven't received anything in return. But you may have swung too far the other way, thinking you don't need to pay dues or give of yourself to earn what you want. Put some of yourself into that relationship. Don't do all the giving. It can be important to let other people give to you so they can invest something of themselves in the relationship too. But for a little while, stop thinking about what you're going to receive—just give. Instead of grumbling about how unfulfilling that job is, maybe you could make it more fulfilling by giving more of yourself. Where you are willing to pay dues can tell you a lot about what you desire. Don't just stand there with one hand in your pocket. Work for what you want.

ᏬᏗ **Day 6** ᏗᏬ

Believing we deserve good things isn't always as easy as simply saying an affirmation like "I believe I deserve." We're often called to pay dues by giving of ourselves. It can tax and strain us at every level. But when we've finally paid the dues, we can better appreciate what we receive.

> **Gratitude Focus:** *We can be grateful each time we have a chance to pay dues. Even if we don't know how valuable it is to feel like we've earned something, our Higher Power does.*

ᏬᏗ **Day 7** ᏗᏬ

"You get what you pay for." "There's no such thing as a free lunch." These sayings have been around for a long time because they are true. There is also another old saying: "The best things in life are free."

The greatest gifts we receive are unmerited blessings from above. We don't pay dues to entice our Higher Power to show favor.

> **Prayer:** *Show me when and where to pay dues. Help me see when enough is enough and it's time to let myself off the hook. Please prepare my heart so I can receive the blessings you have for me.*

Humility

⏣ **Day 1** ⏣

It was an exhilarating week in New York. I did satellite TV interviews that were broadcast all over the United States. I spoke to groups of people and held book signings. The publisher put me up at one of the finest luxury hotels. Then they transported me to the airport in a stretch limousine.

I worked hard, had fun, and was excited to go home. I left the last publicity appointment wearing my dressy work clothes to the airport instead of changing into my jeans. I wore a fancy silk blouse and wraparound skirt. I checked my baggage and made my way to the gate at the end of the corridor to catch my flight to Minneapolis, where I lived at the time.

I don't know whether I can say that all the touring and publicity went to my head, but I was feeling good about myself and my life. I was stepping high and fast. The ticket counter was in sight. I was about an hour and a half early for my flight. As I walked past a group of more than fifty people, most of who were sitting in chairs facing my direction, I felt the strangest feeling around my legs. I took another step, then another. Then I said to myself, "I can't believe this is happening to me." I looked down at the floor. My wraparound skirt had come loose and it was in a tangled heap on the floor.

I looked up briefly, long enough to know I didn't want to make eye contact with the fifty people who were watching. Then I grabbed my skirt and ran. Humility is a delicate thing.

An old-timer in Alcoholics Anonymous used to say, the minute you say you've got it, you've lost it. The claiming of *it*—success, achievement—makes it disappear.

Value: Shhh. *Don't tell anybody. But humility is the value we'll privately and quietly practice all week.*

✐ Day 2 ✐

So, I beg God and beg God to help me do something. I'm in absolute despair. Then I try again, fail, and beg God some more. Finally, I surrender to God's Will. And with God's help, I accomplish what I could not do on my own.

"Look at what I did," I proudly say when I am done.

We can feel good about what we do. But in a do-it-yourself society, a little humility is good. Humility is an honest response to life.

Application: *Don't worry about when to practice humility. If we forget to do it, this value will find us, all on its own.*

✐ Day 3 ✐

God's Will can happen so naturally, beautifully, and power-fully that we forget that our successes and satisfactions are God's doings, not our own.

Challenge: *The most challenging part about practicing*

humility isn't when we do it voluntarily. It's the times we forget to be humble, and it's forced upon us. Think of it as a circle with a line drawn through the middle. On one side of the circle is humility. On the other is pride. If we stay on the pride side, life will push and shove us into the humility side. If we work at staying on the humble side, we may be tempted to go visit pride. But if we do, we'll get pushed right back. There's a fine line between feeling good about ourselves and grateful for our lives, and crossing over into pride. It's worth it to do the work to stay on the humble side of that line. We may still have embarrassing moments, times of being shown our own weaknesses, times when we do what we've just judged someone else for doing. But if we're on the humble side, those things won't bother us nearly as much. We don't practice humility to avoid being humbled. Practicing humility is its own reward.

১৯ Day 4 ৫৬

"No matter how powerful we are, something more powerful than us will always come along," a woman, a mentor of mine, said. "You can be the richest, most powerful person in the world, but you can still break your leg when you fall down the steps."

Many of us have been humbled by forces we couldn't control. It may be the alcoholism or problem of someone else. It may be our own problems with alcohol or other drugs. It may be an illness or a problem that crops up that we can't solve.

Sometimes the best way to practice humility is to say, "I am powerless." Some people take offense at that.

"Women have been powerless long enough" is a common battle cry. Many of us, however, have learned how to delicately embrace the idea of powerlessness. By admitting powerlessness where and when it is appropriate, we become empowered.

__Inventory Focus:__ You can't declare yourself humble. The minute you say you're humble, you're probably not. Whom do you know who demonstrates an admirable combination of both self-esteem and humility, someone you can use as a role model in your life?

ひ Day 5 㐫

When I asked my mentor what we could do to stay humble and at the same time increase our power, her answer was simple: meditation and prayer. Isn't that funny? She's not in a Twelve Step program, but there was the Eleventh Step of Alcoholics Anonymous: "Sought through prayer and meditation to improve our conscious contact with God *as we understood Him,* praying only for knowledge of His will for us and the power to carry that out." Some concepts resonate across all religious and spiritual pursuits.

__Action:__ Beyond practicing regular prayer and meditation, I was told by another mentor that forgetting about yourself and serving others is the very best antidote for pride.

ひ Day 6 㐫

Humility is even necessary and helpful when we talk to God. In the Seventh Step of Alcoholics Anonymous, when we ask God to change us, the Step doesn't say *demand*. It suggests that we *humbly ask*.

Gratitude Focus: *Instead of thinking we should do it ourselves, we can be grateful for every situation that shows us how much we need guidance and help from our Higher Power.*

✍ Day 7 ✍

I put a sign on my wall. This is what the sign says, just in case I forget: "I didn't do it my way. And I didn't do it alone."

Prayer: *Teach me to be as tolerant and forgiving with others as you are with me.*

Perseverance

♥ **Day 1** ↷

"We're born with some values," a friend said. "Others we need to acquire."

"One day at a time" and forgiveness are values I acquired out of necessity. They've been hard won. I'd go through a difficult time and discover each value as a survival tool. Sometimes after a tough experience, I would ask, "What was the value of that?" Later, I would see that from the experience a value, such as compassion or surrender, had worked its way into my life.

These values exist. When we practice them, they become part of us.

By the time I got to chemical dependency treatment in 1973, I had continued to use drugs in the face of all adversity and against all odds. I had begun using other drugs when narcotics were hard to find. Despite everyone screeching at me to stop and being challenged at every level not to drink and use, I continued to get high.

Nothing—not the criminal justice system, the pleadings of people I loved, the consequences my lifestyle created—could cause me to veer from my path. When it didn't look like there was any possible way to get more alcohol and drugs, I found them. I even woke up in an emergency room, suffering from an overdose, where I ripped off cardiac monitors and headed for the exit screaming, "I want more!" When I went into treatment, I still found ways, although they weren't very impressive, to chemically change how I felt.

When things began turning around for me in treatment, when I began considering another way of life, I had to do an inventory and tell someone my shameful secrets. By then I decided that if I put even half the energy into doing the right thing as I'd invested in doing the wrong thing, there was little I couldn't do. I worked hard at my inventory. I was able to come up with a lot of character defects, moral deficiencies, and flaws. The clergyperson I talked to listened carefully. When he asked whether I could see anything good about myself, I said no.

"I can," he said. "You are persistent. In the face of all odds, you have a remarkable ability to persevere."

Most of our values are acquired through hard work. But once in a while we get a free one. We don't have to work at it. At least not that hard. Like in the game of Monopoly, we get a card that tells us to advance to "Go" and collect $200.

Being persistent is the one value that comes naturally to me. I thank God for that.

Value: Perseverance is the value this week. Perseverance has many faces: staying with a thing in the face of all odds, trying again and again, trying harder, figuring out how to overcome opposition no matter how creative we need to get, crawling over broken glass to accomplish our goals, going to any lengths even when we'd rather not.

✌ **Day 2** ➳

Now we're getting the hang of it. Sometimes we don't need to completely learn a new trick to apply these values in our lives. We just need to take something we already do, turn it around, and make that thing work for us.

Application: Whenever we get obsessed with doing things our way, it's a good time to refocus that energy and persevere in surrendering to—and doing—God's Will.

✌ **Day 3** ➳

I have a friend who had been sober for a while, then he started using again. For a period of years, no matter how hard he tried, he couldn't get back on track. Finally he was able to get sober again, but he didn't take it for granted. He was scared. Hope was a fragile quality in his life.

I, too, know that feeling. After my son died, the waves of grief kept washing over me, year after year. Sometimes I didn't know whether it was worth it, waking up each day to that ongoing pain. You, too, have probably experienced prolonged periods of fear or pain. It's not that we don't want good things in our lives; it's just so difficult to rekindle hope when we have lost it.

Challenge: If there is a reccurring, nagging problem in our lives right now, we can identify it. We can then tell ourselves, "No matter how many times I have tried and failed to fix this, I can still try one more time." Many of us have tried fixing relationships that didn't have a remote chance of working. But now, how about turning it around and persevering toward the good stuff in your life?

Day 4

"I know my limitations," a friend said. "Point me in a direction, and I'll just keep walking no matter what." Maybe we could take a minute and evaluate what we're moving toward?

Inventory Focus: Have you ever tried to do the impossible in your life, like trying to control someone else's behavior instead of gaining manageability of yourself? Ever done the same thing over and over, even though what you were doing will never work? See! You already know how to persevere. Take a moment. Decide to make this trait work for you. Persevere at applying chosen values in your life.

Day 5

"Please hire me for this job," I said to the publisher of the daily newspaper.

"I can't. You don't have a degree," he said.

I went back weekly for months. Finally one day he said yes. Sometimes it's not the person with the most talent who succeeds. It's the person who keeps showing up.

Action: After I wrote my first book, I kept a huge cardboard carton of all the mistakes, trials and errors, and pages I didn't use in the completed manuscript. By the time we become successful, we've done a thing for years—whether it's recovery, writing, practicing our values, or anything else. Successful people make a thing look easy and effortless. Remind yourself and others how hard success really is.

"My son had a learning disability," his father said.

"When he asked whether he should go to college, I said yes, he'd just have to work harder than most everyone else. He did. He just got his Ph.D."

When you can't make the obstacles go away, use them as leverage to push against.

✒ **Day 6** ✒

"My relationship and marriage was hard from day one," a woman said. "We've been together five years now. I don't think it was until year four that we finally fell in love and learned what love is about."

Thank God for the real challenges in life.

Gratitude Focus: *A lot of times we persevere and fail. We can be grateful for failures. We learn from them too. And we can be grateful when our perseverance finally pays off.*

✒ **Day 7** ✒

"Why do we keep climbing mountains when it's so hard and we spend so little time at the top?" I asked my hiking partner. "Because we're not doing it just for those moments at the top. That's so we have someplace to go. What most people don't get, and what we need to remember, is that the climb is the important part."

Prayer: *Please give me the stamina to persevere in doing your Will. Teach me the difference between giving up and letting go. Whenever I get discouraged, please send me guidance and hope.*

Generosity

☙ Day 1 ❧

During my second trip to Tibet, I made a journey to Mount Kailesh, considered by many to be the holiest mountain there. It took almost a week just to get from Lhasa to the mountain. The tour guide, Lami, had made this journey before. He knew guesthouses and hotels along the way to rest and spend the night.

During the course of Lami's many trips to this sacred mountain, he had gotten to know the innkeepers. Some of them were friends from another time in his life. Others were new acquaintances. Lami was particularly excited to reach a particular hotel and visit with the innkeeper, a man he called "his close friend."

The first thing we did when we got to the hotel was meet in the dining room. The innkeeper kept commenting on Lami's jacket. It was a newly purchased shiny blue windbreaker that was light but guaranteed warmth.

"No wonder the innkeeper keeps touching the jacket and talking about it," I thought. "Lami looks so good in it."

The next morning, we all met in the dining room for breakfast. Lami was no longer wearing his shiny jacket. He wore a tattered plaid jacket instead. The plaid jacket wasn't just old; it was too small.

When the innkeeper walked into the room, he was wearing a smile on his face and Lami's shiny blue jacket.

"What happened?" I asked Lami. "Why is he wearing your jacket? Did you sell it to him?"

At first, Lami grimaced while he explained, "In my country, we have a custom," he said. "When a friend asks for something you have, it is important to give him whatever he wants. It's important, if possible, to say yes."

Lami looked at the innkeeper and gave his blue jacket a lingering good-bye look. Then his grimace turned into a smile. "This jacket is fine," he said. "It'll keep me warm. And my friend looks good wearing his new jacket, don't you think?"

"How codependent," I thought to myself at first. "But maybe it's not," I thought after a while.

When we returned to Lhasa after visiting the holy mountain, I saw Lami wearing another new jacket. It was as nice or nicer than the one he had given away.

It's important to say no. Most of us have learned that the hard way. But we can say no—and hang on to things—a little too much sometimes.

Value: Generosity is the value this week.

∽ Day 2 ∾

Generosity doesn't only mean giving money. It's both an attitude and a behavior we demonstrate toward others and ourselves. It includes smiling, listening, giving compliments, forgiving, being compassionate, being kind, laughing, approving, mentoring, encouraging—being generous with all the good stuff in life.

Application: Sometimes saying no is an important thing to do. But if we're habitually withholding all the good stuff—trying to keep it for ourselves and finding we have less and less instead of more—we might want to try loosening up and being generous instead.

⟿ Day 3 ⟿

He worked in a social services office. One night, at the close of the day, a young woman wandered in. She was newly sober, had nowhere to go, and didn't have a penny in her pocket. "I told her she could use the phones to try to get some help," he said. "I wanted to do something for her, give her some money—some practical help. But I had such strong codependency issues that I had worked on that I was afraid it was wrong to give. I know it's not my fault or my responsibility, but I wish now that I had given more."

Some of us gave way too much, way too often, in the wrong places. We gave and gave to black holes, or we gave in such a way that people became dependent on us and didn't take responsibility for themselves. Or we gave when we really didn't want to. When we looked in our heart and searched, the real answer was no.

It's not giving that's bad. Giving is good. Some of us get confused and think giving is wrong. It's only time to stop giving and take care of ourselves when we give compulsively, give obsessively, squander our resources in an irresponsible way, confuse giving with grandiosity, or give in a way that enables and harms.

Once we learn how to say no, we learn that it's equally valuable to learn when to say yes.

Challenge: *The hardest thing about giving can be determining when what we're doing is healthy giving and when it's not. We may be afraid of being manipulated and used if we walk around the world with a generous spirit. That happens sometimes. Maybe we will get manipulated or tricked once in a while, but I don't think that's a* codependent *slip. Sometimes it's time to back off from giving and just take care of ourselves. That's only part of recovering and mental health. After we do that, it's time to get back in the game and learn how and when to give.*

✍ Day 4 ✍

I know, giving can hurt. Grimace if you must. But sometimes the generous thing isn't just the giving. It's giving with a blessing and a smile.

Inventory Focus: *Evaluate all your resources, not just your material assets. What have you been given? Whatever we want to keep is probably what we need to give away.*

✍ Day 5 ✍

We don't want to overextend ourselves. And we need to consider our commitments carefully. But it doesn't hurt any of us once in a while to loosen up and say yes.

Action: *Sometimes it's okay to give people what they ask for and want. It's okay to be generous with yourself too. Don't just give what you'd like to receive. If you decide to give, consider giving people what they want.*

༄ **Day 6** ༄

Mine and *no.* Good words. So are *this is for you* and *yes.* We can be especially grateful once we've learned to say no because now we mean it when we say yes.

Gratitude Focus: *We can be grateful for each opportunity to generously give.*

༄ **Day 7** ༄

Since that trip to Tibet, I have reevaluated my giving. On a couple occasions, when I knew someone really admired a possession that belonged to me, I gave it to that person. "Here, you can have it," I said. "It's yours." The look of amazement on their faces when I said it was nothing compared to what I felt.

Generosity is the value we practice. Nonattachment is a gift.

Prayer: *Guide me about when and how to give. Help me live with a generous spirit toward others and myself. Thank you for all the generosity you've shown me.*

Commitment

☙ **Day 1** ❧

Who or what are you committed to, through good times and bad? What person or value do you cherish most? For a long time, the only thing I was committed to was using drugs. I began to learn about the value of commitment in treatment in 1973. The treatment facility suggested that I make the same commitment to sobriety that I had to using chemicals—take life one day at a time, but commit to sobriety no matter what.

Almost thirty years later, I was walking through my house, getting ready to do errands. Out of nowhere, the thought came to me. "I'd really like someone to take care of me for a change."

"Well who wouldn't," I thought back to myself. Taking care of ourselves can be an overwhelming and exhausting job.

When I married my children's father, I had some fantasies. I wanted a husband who would be a good provider. I would be a good wife. But I wanted someone to take care of me. As the years wore on and I wore out from taking care of everyone around me and not taking care of myself, I saw that that wasn't going to happen. If I took care of everyone around me and didn't take care of

231

myself, nobody was going to notice and say, "Oh, look. Someone needs to take care of her."

I was going to die—or get bitter—from neglect. I had made commitments to everyone around me—sobriety, my children, my husband—but I had forgotten to make a commitment to taking care of myself.

Sometimes commitments are a lifetime deal. We say I'm going to keep doing this, no matter what. Other times a commitment is a temporary one-time pledge of our energy or time. God willing, I'll do this task, no matter what.

Many of us have found occasion to make a commitment, then change our mind. We thought a particular commitment would be good for us. But then that commitment conflicted with another commitment we had made.

Commitments can make some of us panic. Have you ever gotten cold feet after making a committed decision, such as buying a new house?

Commitments—big or small—require follow-through. Once we say "I do" or "I will," it's our job to either complete the task or let someone know we can't. Some of our happiest moments come after going through the cold feet thing and still keeping our word. Some of the hardest choices we have to make are when we change our mind and say, "I'm sorry, I can't."

Value: The dreaded C word—*commitment*—is the value this week.

༄ Day 2 ༄

"I had such a hard time with commitment that I couldn't complete a task," a woman said. "It all manifested in how

I did the dishes. No matter how hard I tried, I always left two or three dirty dishes in the sink. Once I learned about this (my therapist called it *completing the transaction*), I was ready to move on to bigger and braver things, like getting married and having kids."

Big commitments are important in life. But committing to smaller tasks is important too. Returning phone calls, getting tasks completed, showing up when we pledge our presence are all important commitments. Making a commitment to our recovery group is important. When we're able to follow through on our commitments, other people value our word and we have more esteem.

Application: Whenever possible, we need to do what we say we will. If we can't muster up to the big commitments, we can start small.

ᴇᴠᴀ **Day 3** ᴀᴠᴡ

Have you ever made a commitment and immediately realized you'd made a mistake? It was more than just cold feet. You had promised to do something you knew you couldn't do.

One of the challenges with commitments is human error. We change our mind. It could be that we didn't think things through. Or maybe one commitment we made interfered with another important pledge. For instance, if we're married to someone who is on a destructive path, our commitment to that person might interfere with the commitment we've made to our children and to ourselves.

The idea of committing is often easier than fulfilling the commitment itself. Many of the things we commit to, such as raising children, require hard work.

Challenge: The hard thing about commitments isn't making them. It's following through. Commitments require consideration—which ones to make, which ones to break, which ones to complete. It's serious business, this commitment thing.

✐ Day 4 ✐

After my son died, I began to lose my will to live. I sat down and wrote out an unconditional commitment to life. It was one of the most freeing things I did. I didn't have to waver in my commitment from that moment on. I don't know whether life cared or not about the agreement I made, but making that commitment helped me.

Inventory Focus: What commitments have you made so far in your life? How do you feel about them now? How did you feel when you made them? Do you have a problem with overcommitting yourself? Have you ever had to break a commitment? If you can't fulfill your commitments, which sometimes happens, at least you can be responsible enough to tell someone you can't.

✐ Day 5 ✐

Sometimes we only need to commit to something or someone once and that commitment lasts for life. Other times it helps to renew our vows. Committing to sobriety, values, or self-care and responsibility is a decision we can make each day.

Action: Carefully weigh your pledges. Take time to think things through. A commitment is a contract. Once you commit, it means you're going to do a thing whether you feel like it or not. Try to make commitments only to those things you truly care about. Knowing when not to commit is important too.

Whenever you commit, your energy and resources will follow.

ᘓ **Day 6** ᘖ

Thank God when we believe in a person or an idea enough to finally commit.

Gratitude Focus: *We can be grateful whenever we make and fulfill a commitment, whether it's to a person, to a task, to a job, or to ourselves. When we get off that fence, we know where we stand.*

ᘓ **Day 7** ᘖ

Saying "I will" is a powerful thing. It carves a path through life.

Prayer: *Please guide me in making commitments. Teach me that my commitments guide my life. Help me be gentle with others and myself when I need to renege on commitments. Whenever and as much as possible, give me strength to follow through.*

Vulnerable Honesty

ᮢ Day 1 ᮡ

Him: "I'd like to see you tonight."

Her: "I'd like to see you too, but I need to work. I miss you a lot, and if I had a preference, I'd rather be with you."

Him: "I'd like to see you tonight."

Her: "I told you I'm busy. Can't you respect my needs?"

There's a fine line between being vulnerably honest and *just being honest.* Has a friend ever called early in the morning, right when you were waking up? Can you remember how you talked then, before your defenses were up?

When we're vulnerably honest, our defenses are down. We're gentler, kinder, more open about ourselves. When people preface whatever they're going to say with "I'm just being honest," they're usually going to tell us what they think. Vulnerability doesn't need a preface or an introduction. It comes from the heart, and it speaks for itself.

A man was complaining about something I'd said in one of my books. "Don't you know people will read that and interpret it as encouragement to do anything they want, maybe have an affair and cheat on their husband?"

he said. "Or if they're recovering, they'll think it's okay to get high again?"

I started to respond by being defensive. Then I took a deep breath and went into my heart. I explained that that was never my intention. I wondered whether he had possibly misinterpreted it? Then I took an even deeper breath and took a chance. "Are you in a lot of pain?" I asked.

It didn't take him long to respond. "Yes, I am in pain. Thank you for asking," he said. "I just discovered my wife had an affair, and I don't know what to do."

When we get those defenses down and come from the heart, it doesn't just help us. It helps other people open up too.

Value: Honesty, the vulnerable kind, is the value this week.

∽ Day 2 ∾

Honesty is the best policy. But sometimes vulnerable honesty is better yet.

Application: It's not always appropriate to be vulnerably honest. But when we start practicing it, we'll be surprised how much more often it's appropriate than it's not.

∽ Day 3 ∾

Vulnerable honesty is a powerful thing. When we're vulnerable and honest, people respond well to it. Vulnerable dishonesty can be powerful too. It looks and feels like vulnerable honesty, but it's a manipulation device. We think someone's opening their heart to us, but they're not. It's an enchantment being used to manipulate us. The problem is, once we respond by opening our heart, it can be hard to tell whether we're being lied to or not.

Sometimes when we're going through an extended period of pain, such as battling depression or a chronic problem, we may get tired of sharing how we feel. We may think, "Why would anyone else want to hear who I really am? I don't even want to hear about it myself."

We may have been hurt by being vulnerable before. Then we made a decision, a choice. "I'm never going to let anyone hurt me again." Not being vulnerable doesn't mean we won't get hurt. Whether we like it or not, taking the risk to love anyone puts us in a vulnerable place.

Defensiveness protects us but it also pushes people away. Vulnerability pulls people in. How about taking a risk and letting some of those tender feelings show?

Challenge: *The hardest thing about vulnerable honesty for me is getting out of my head and into my heart, trusting myself—not other people—to say who I really am. Sometimes I'm so used to being strong that I don't even recognize vulnerable feelings. What's the hardest thing for you? Go ahead. Try practicing vulnerability. It grows on us after a while.*

✍ Day 4 ✍

Before we can be honest with anyone else, we need to be honest with ourselves.

Inventory Focus: *How do you do with sharing the tender part of you, the soft spot in your heart? Do you let yourself acknowledge feelings such as missing someone, wanting to be with them, or feeling hurt? When you* *get sad or frightened, how do you handle it? Many people suggest that underneath exteriors of being cranky, cold, or mean is a person who feels scared, betrayed, guilty, or hurt. Maybe you could let some of those defenses go and not protect yourself quite as much?*

ᏯᏯ **Day 5** ᏯᏯ

The first time I practiced vulnerable honesty was many years ago. I was talking to a clergyperson. I was going over a list of shortcomings and things I'd done wrong. When I finished, he just looked at me. "What else?" he asked.

"Nothing," I said.

"What else?" he repeated.

I felt like the world was going to rip apart. "I want to stay sober, but I don't know how and I don't think I can," I said. Vulnerable honesty opened up my world at that moment.

Action: Being vulnerable and honest takes a little more time and effort than being a talking head. What we're really talking about with vulnerable honesty is opening our heart. It's easy to say, "I'm irritable." It's a little tougher to say, "My hands are trembling, and I'm scared." Just peel off one more layer. There, that's it. See how beautiful that heart is?

One way to put vulnerable honesty into practice is to stop thinking about what you should say and really listen and respond to the other person. Another way is to say how you really feel.

If it's difficult to be vulnerably honest, try this approach. After you finish talking to someone, take a moment. Did you skip saying something important that might have made you feel vulnerable and the other person feel good? Or maybe the reverse applies. Are you not expressing your emotional truth because you don't want to hurt someone, or be that vulnerable, or because you suspect your feelings are wrong?

You don't have to fawn and gush, but instead of keeping those delicate feelings to yourself, you can share them with others and let them know how much they mean to you. That one sweet vulnerable thing you say might be the thing that lights up their day.

✧ Day 6 ✧

Thank God being cold, harsh, brass, and flippant is finally on the way to becoming passé. Vulnerable honesty is coming back in style.

Gratitude Focus: *We can be grateful whenever we catch ourselves being defensive, when we take the time to be vulnerable instead. We'll learn to combine vulnerability with taking care of ourselves. Guaranteed. There's a lot more strength in vulnerability than there is in force. And the two can be combined.*

✧ Day 7 ✧

We don't have to run around the world dripping feelings. But every once in a while, a little sugar is nice.

Prayer: *Teach me the power of words that come from my heart.*

Perspective

✒ **Day 1** ✒

Whenever other people say we've got to keep things in perspective, I wonder whose perspective they're talking about—mine or theirs. Perspective is more than a point of view. It's looking at things closely and looking from a distance.

Sometimes what immediately appears to be a full-blown crisis later becomes a minor problem. Even later on, our perspective may change again. What was at first a full-blown crisis, then a problem, later becomes a blessing.

Most of us have taken pictures with a camera. We can photograph something from different angles and different distances. The same object can look entirely different from far away than it does up close.

Sometimes we watch a friend, loved one, acquaintance, or stranger experiencing a problem. We may judge them, think it's ridiculous, or not understand. Later on in life, when we find ourselves experiencing that problem, we begin to see it differently. That's because we're seeing it up close.

There was a time when my point of view was the only way I saw each scene. When we watch a movie or read a book, we usually hear the story told from one person's point of view. When we're living our lives, we can get that way too. As we're working our way through all the scenes that make up our destiny, we can narrowly think the only main character is us and the only real point of view is ours.

We each have different backgrounds, histories, intentions, goals, hopes, and dreams. We each have different feelings. We have different levels of history to draw on in our problem-solving skills. And each of us has at least a slightly different approach to life.

We don't see things as they are, we see things as we are—at any point in time.

Value: Perspective is the value this week.

Day 2

Zoom in. Zoom out. Then try looking at the conversation or the situation from another point of view.

Application: Whenever we find ourselves overreacting, we may want to zoom out a bit. Whenever we find ourselves underreacting or being accused of living in denial, it may help to zoom in to see the details and then zoom out and see whether there's a pattern going on. Whenever we find ourselves in conflict, we may want to take a minute and look at both sides.

Day 3

When we're in high-drama mode, everything is a crisis. But that's often because we need the adrenalin or we're bored.

Perspective acknowledges that the other person has a point of view. And it says that how he or she views the situation is as valid to them as our point of view is to us. But a problem can arise when we practice too much perspective: we begin only to see the other point of view and forget that our point of view matters too.

Don't assume that others are feeling how we'd be feeling if we were them. That's not perspective. It's naively assuming the other person is just like us.

The ability to get into other people's heads, see things their way, and acknowledge the validity of their point of view is a learned skill that takes practice and time.

Challenge: The hardest thing about perspective is it means we need to grow up. Or maybe we don't. One way to have good perspective is to see the world through the eyes of a child. We innocently report. We accept how others think and feel. If something is bad or sad, or we're scared, we say that. We say how we feel and what we want and need. We know that when we're tired, we see things out of focus. And when things get too difficult, we either go play in the park or we take a nap. Somehow we know that everything will work out.

∽ Day 4 ∾

What a boring world it would be if we all saw everything the same.

Inventory Focus: Are you struggling to gain perspective on something right now? Wise people suggest sleeping on things when you're confused. Or counting to ten when you get mad. That's because they know that perspective is apt to quickly change how you see things.

∽ **Day 5** ∾

The most practical way to practice perspective is to let ourselves see things as we do, knowing that in ten minutes or three hours, how we see things is likely to change.

Action: Don't just ask yourself what other people's perspectives are. Ask them. Men often see things differently than women. Children see things differently than adults. Two years is half a lifetime to a four-year-old. It's a moment in time to someone sixty years old. Going through certain experiences changes how you see things. When you're bitter, you see things one way. When you have hope, you see things in a different light. Don't expect someone in excruciating pain to keep things in perspective. They probably can't. All they know is that it hurts.

When a problem arises, here's a trick old-timers in Alcoholics Anonymous teach. Will this problem still matter and be a crisis a year from now? Give yourself and others time for perspective to change. Life has a way of shifting itself around. Even if you can't get something in perspective right now, if you stay open, life has a way of doing that for you. Talk to other people. Hearing what others have to say is a good way to gain perspective when you can't get things in focus on your own. That's why people in recovery share their experience, strength, and hope.

The real trick to perspective is combining it with respect and tolerance. Remember, each person thinks he or she is the main character in the story—and that he or she is the only one who counts.

ᏬᏯ **Day 6** ᏭᏀ

We can practice perspective on our lessons too. We may think we're learning and working out one thing in life, only to discover later that we were learning something else.

Gratitude Focus: *We can be grateful for the people who help us keep things in perspective when we can't do it ourselves. When all attempts to put things in perspective fail, seeing things in the light of gratitude helps.*

ᏬᏯ **Day 7** ᏭᏀ

Blow it up way out of proportion. Now shrink it down until it's tiny in size. See how it's going to look in six months or a year from now. We don't have to wait for life to bring things into perspective. Stretch that imagination. Bring some perspective into the situation right now.

Prayer: *Help me remember that everything looks better when I trust you. Remind me that there's a larger story being told than the tiny part I can see now.*

WEEK 50

Compassion

Day 1

I met one of my friends at an odd time in my life. I had just moved to California from Minnesota. I was in the early years of my grief after the death of my son, Shane. My daughter, Nichole, had turned eighteen. She was moving to New York. I had a lot of change going on. I knew who I had been and what my life was like. But I didn't know what it was going to become.

My friend was in a transition period in his life too. He'd mention bits and pieces of the changes he had gone through. A marriage that hadn't worked out. Getting stuck alone in what he thought was going to be the home of his dreams. He was uncertain of where he fit and where he belonged.

We had a lot of good times together during those transition years, just hanging out with each other and our other friends. We sensed all these things about each other —that the other person was going through grief, loss, change, and had a lot of uncertainty going on. But it wasn't until years later that we really understood. We were having lunch together. By then he had remarried and had his first child. I had adjusted to Shane being gone and to Nichole being married and having children of her own.

We were both on more solid ground.

"I never really understood how much pain you were in then," he said. "I'd watch you go about your life. I'd hear you talk about parts of what you'd been through, but I didn't understand the way I do now."

"Ditto," I said. "When you talked about your divorce and the things going on in your life, I understood intellectually that you had been through a lot of trauma and change. But I didn't understand—not really—what a hard time that was in your life."

Sometimes when we meet other people—and even after we've gotten to know them—all we see is the tip of the iceberg when we look at their lives. We don't understand the things that are driving them, the unresolved issues from their pasts, and the depth of pain they're in now.

We don't want to have so much compassion that we enable others to hurt themselves or trod down the wrong path. And we don't want to overunderstand, which is understanding the other person so much that we don't take care of or understand ourselves.

But it doesn't hurt to look a little deeper after a first glance.

Value: Having healthy compassion for other people and ourselves is the value this week.

∽ Day 2 ∼

I met her at a party at a friend's house. I introduced myself. We chatted a little. I went on my way. Later I learned that her husband of ten years had just died a few months before, leaving her alone with three children.

"Why didn't you tell me?" I asked my friend.

"What was I going to do—introduce her as *the newly bereaved?* Besides, she wants everyone to think she's strong."

I said it before. I'll say it again. I think our society should let us wear signs: *Fragile. Broken Heart. Handle with Care.*

Application: *Don't worry about when to apply the value of compassion. If we stick around long enough, compassion will find us.*

∽ Day 3 ∾

It can be difficult to tell when we cross the line from compassion to overcaring—understanding another person *so much* that we don't hold them accountable for what they do.

There are a lot of lines we can cross with compassion. We can move into pity for others or ourselves. But going too far the other way isn't good either. We can be so hard on others and ourselves that we don't allow for normal feelings of sadness and grief.

Challenge: *The hardest thing about having compassion is that often we truly don't understand how a thing feels until we wake up one day and it happens to us.*

∽ Day 4 ∾

Here's another quirk some of us have. We're able to demonstrate a lot of compassion for other people. We can understand why they did the things they did. But when we look in that mirror, we can't seem to muster up any compassion, forgiveness, or understanding for ourselves.

Inventory Focus: *Expecting responsible behaviors from*

other people and yourself is a healthy ideal. Maybe you could trust yourself to show compassion and hold others and yourself accountable too?

✐ Day 5 ✐

One of the most compassionate acts ever done toward me was when a district court judge in Minnesota sentenced me to treatment instead of jail for my chemical-dependency-related crimes. I had a jail sentence hanging over my head if I didn't get sober, but he gave me a chance.

Another compassionate act done toward me was when, after I completed treatment, the owner of a law firm agreed to give me a chance at a secretarial job.

Throughout my life, people whom I've hurt have forgiven me and shown compassion too. Giving people a second chance (with limits) and showing forgiveness aren't all that compassion is. But they're a good place to start.

Action: I don't know the rules for being a compassionate person. I'd say don't judge, but most of us judge sometimes, even when we know we're doing the same thing we judged in someone else.

Sometimes it helps just to listen. Ask people questions about themselves. Let them talk.

Pitying myself never helps. But no matter what I'm going through, it helps when other people say, "I understand because I've been there too. I got through it and I know you will too."

In the Big Book of Alcoholics Anonymous, it says that if you keep cleaning your side of the street and surrendering to a Higher Power, you'll grow to not regret the past because even the worst things will be put to good use. You'll be able to use your mistakes and flaws to help someone else.

The best way to practice healthy compassion is to be willing to have an open heart and let life and your Higher Power work in you.

∽ Day 6 ∾

Thank God for people who believe in us.

Gratitude Focus: *We can be grateful that no matter what we're going through, someone else has gone through it and can share their experience, strength, and hope. Instead of regretting our mistakes, we can be grateful that we have special experiences, strength, and hope to share with someone else.*

∽ Day 7 ∾

Go through your experiences. Discover what compassion means to you.

Prayer: *Give me the courage to be honest with myself and others about who I am and what I am going through. Please help me keep believing in other people and myself.*

Meditation

ᴗᴥ Day 1 ᴥᴗ

The first time I heard about meditation, it sounded like a foreign concept to me. I could understand prayer. That was talking to God. It made sense. But people said meditation was important too. Someone told me, "That's when you're being quiet, so God can talk to you."

Over the years, I've been exposed to different kinds of meditation. There's walking meditation, reading out of a meditation book, and meditation where we sit on the floor with our legs crossed and eyes closed while chanting "om."

I still feel intimidated when other people ask me about meditation. It's one of those things I don't feel I do enough, and when I do, I have a lingering sense that I'm not doing it right. But if you ask me whether I try to spend time quieting myself, getting centered, becoming relieved of my own tiresome, worrisome, obsessive thoughts each day, the answer is absolutely yes.

I started my meditation practice by reading daily out of a little black book called *Twenty-Four Hours a Day*. After spending several years with that, I switched to *God Calling*.

As time went on, I began to study different, more formalized practices. The martial art I study, aikido, is considered a walking and moving meditation. It's also considered a spiritual martial art. Meditation practice is part of training. As a result of that art, I learned to sit on the floor, with legs crossed and eyes shut, and be quiet for a while. In the beginning, five minutes was about my limit for sitting still. After that, I'd start opening my eyes and peeking around the room to see what other people were doing.

Later on, I added yoga to my repertoire of meditative practices. It's a workout, but it's also spiritually centering and includes meditation. I was intimidated for years about trying yoga. It was another one of those things I was certain I couldn't do well enough. I thought it was one of those things for other people, but not for me. Eventually I found myself in a class. I found people of all age groups stretching, trying to hold poses, doing the best they could.

I've sat in the pyramids of Egypt and meditated. I've sat next to the Dead Sea and the Sea of Galilee with eyes closed, trying to be quiet. I've sat next to the sacred Mount Kailesh in Tibet, cross-legged, eyes closed, holding the pose for almost an hour. Sometimes when I close my eyes I pray. Sometimes I try to focus on a meditative thought. Usually I try to focus on breathing and being as still as I can.

I'm not sure that it matters where or how we meditate, or whether we cross our legs, chant "om," or read an idea out of a book. The important idea with meditation is this: Be still so we can hear God.

Value: Meditation is the value this week.

～ Day 2 ～

"I need to run on my treadmill while I meditate," a friend

said. "I've got to do something to distract my mind."

Sometimes I like to play soothing or spiritual music to keep my mind occupied.

Keep it simple. What helps you calm down and relax?

Application: Some of us like to meditate first thing in the morning. Others of us prefer the afternoon or night. This value can be applied regularly and as needed. If getting tense, fearful, and obsessed isn't helping, how about meditating instead?

⸙ Day 3 ⸙

It's easy to tell ourselves we're too busy, already overloaded, don't have time to be still. If we're already too busy and stressed, how can taking more time out of our schedule to do one more thing possibly help? Taking five minutes to be still, focus on a positive thought, or formally meditate can get us almost immediately back on track. I don't know how meditation works, but it does.

Challenge: There's nothing hard about meditating. Take a deep breath. Now take another one. Try to relax those shoulders a little. We don't have to work at things quite so hard. Let God's power work through us.

⸙ Day 4 ⸙

Many of us have an altar in our home. On it, we keep spiritual or religious objects. We're supposed to keep our altar clean, tended, well kept. I like to burn candles and incense on mine. The spiritual space we're trying to find and maintain in meditation practice is the sacred place in each of us.

Inventory Focus: What are your meditation practices? Have you found that space, the one inside each of us, that transcends space and time? It's there. And no matter what's going on around us, it's quiet there. After we've been in that space for a few minutes, we're restored. We can gently get up, return to our lives, and almost effortlessly do what needs to be done.

∾ Day 5 ∾

"Just for a little while, stop thinking about all the problems, crises, tasks, everything that's pulling and pushing on us. Be in that quiet space." I love it when my yoga instructor says that to us. After all these years, some of us still need permission to let go.

Action: The busier and more hectic your life is, the greater the need to meditate. The more you meditate, the calmer and quieter your life is because you're quieter and calmer.

You can be open and flexible in your meditation practices. Maintaining a regular routine is helpful, but sometimes you may need a little more. If you feel so inclined, try something new. Get some books at the library or bookstore, or go on-line. Explore different techniques. Or don't. Stick with whatever works for you. It's your sacred space. You can decorate it however you'd like. What is important is that it's comfortable for you.

∾ Day 6 ∾

Thank God meditation is easier than I convince myself it is. In communication, it takes only a few simple behaviors to hear the other person. We need to stop talking. And we need to listen, preferably with an open heart. No, we don't *hear* God talking to us. But silence speaks louder than words.

Gratitude Focus: *We can be grateful for all the people, reminders, and tools that help us meditate. Meditation is a kind thing to do for ourselves.*

∾ Day 7 ∾

When you cook dinner, notice how good it smells. When you look in the mirror, see how much better you look. That task that was so difficult before is doable now. See! That phone call wasn't an interruption. It was just what you needed. Maybe God isn't just talking to us during meditation time. Maybe the meditation time is so we can get quiet. Then we can hear God talking all day long.

Prayer: *Help me learn to be still so I can hear and feel you throughout the day.*

The Puzzle of Love

~ Day 1 ~

"I'm trying to figure out how to open my heart, and I can't," I said to a friend.

"Puzzling, isn't it?" he replied.

Sometimes it's so hard to get into our heart, so hard to believe that we're lovable and that our love and presence are important in this world.

Most of us have heard the word *love* most of our lives. Our parents told us they loved us. And whether their behavior matched their words or not, most of us wanted to believe that they did.

Then we had that best friend growing up. And how about that teenage crush, and that first kiss? Who can forget that? Oh yeah, then there's that getting-the-heart-broken stuff. That hurts.

A woman I know lost her son during his teenage years. "At least he lived long enough to experience falling in love," she said.

By the time we get a little older, most of us have had a variety of experiences with love. We've experienced some sort of it in our family, with our friends, and in romance too. Other people tell us God loves us. But for those of us who have had histories of painful experiences with love, that can be confusing. We're not sure what it means.

Some of us went the opposite way from love during our teenage and adult years. Instead of loving ourselves, we began destroying ourselves with alcohol and other drugs. Others of us lost ourselves in love, getting hooked into relationships that just didn't work. Then we were lucky enough to get into recovery, and we began to experience a new kind of love. And throughout this whole path, we've kept wondering, "Is love real?" If we have children, we know it is. I've heard from so many people, "I never really understood what love meant until I had a child." Love has never taken the shape and form I thought it should or would.

I have a friend who's a jigsaw puzzle fanatic. She loves sitting and working on a puzzle. The more pieces the better. She enjoys every moment of it, from looking at the picture on the box, to dumping a heap of tiny pieces into a pile, to sorting through them, to finding through trial and error which ones fit where.

Sometimes that's what love feels like, a big puzzle we're trying to put together. Only we don't know what the picture on the cover looks like. And we have to get the pieces one at a time as we go along.

Value: Putting together the puzzle of love is the value this week.

◈ Day 2 ◈

A friend calls. We pick up the phone. And that friend tells us how important we are to him or her. Or a family member calls and expresses his or her love. Or we have a quiet conversation with someone we work with. And beyond any work conflicts or disagreements that might have come up, we feel a connection there. Something touches us. Our heart opens. And we know love is real.

Application: This value happens by the grace of God. Some of us spent our whole lives looking for love—from God, other people, family members. When the lights come on and we finally realize that this is it, it's a pretty amazing thing. Love just didn't look like we thought it would. Love might be a feeling and a gift, but it's also hard work.

⏎ Day 3 ⏎

So other people don't love us the way we wanted to be loved. And we have conflicts and disagreements to work out. And there's that whole forgiveness thing. And sometimes harmonizing with other people can be tricky.

What about when we have to put all that energy into setting boundaries, into telling other people no? And then there's that whole letting go thing, knowing we can't control. That's work. And it sometimes hurts.

And some of those crazy people we thought we were in love with? We look back and wonder what was the value in that? But it prepared these beautiful hearts for love that could really work.

Okay, how about this challenge? We love someone with all our heart and soul, as much or more as we've loved anyone our whole lives. Then they die. They go away. And we don't get to see them, touch them, hear their beautiful voice again.

You don't have to tell me about the challenges of love. I've experienced them all.

Challenge: All through this book, we've talked about the challenges to applying each of the values we've discussed. All those challenges—and more—apply to putting together the puzzle we call love.

ᴄᴀ **Day 4** ᴀᴠ

Are you willing to be a warrior? Are you willing to collect those pieces of your heart and of love as you go along—even when they don't make any sense at all?

Inventory Focus: Can you trust that there's a beautiful picture coming together, even when you don't know what that picture is? It's been said by every holy book, religion, and psychiatrist worth his or her degree: the goal of the spiritual path is love.

ᴄᴀ **Day 5** ᴀᴠ

At the beginning of this year, we talked about going on a treasure hunt and looking for values. Some of them would be gained the hard way. Some handed to us by a friend. Some would be worked out in us as a result of going through tough, sometimes painful circumstances in our lives. We also talked about how important it is to remember that once we get handed a value, it's because we're going to need to use it, probably all our lives. We talked about how important it is to actually practice these values. Just reading about them is like reading a book about exercise. It doesn't do any good until we apply the ideas in our lives.

Action: It's hard to work on the value of love. It's tougher yet to open your heart. But doing your best to work on—and live by—your values is something you can do.

ᑌᑌ **Day 6** ᑌᑌ

Thank God when a piece to that puzzle of love finally fits.

Gratitude Focus: *We can be grateful that we're giving the love we always wanted to get.*

ᑌᑌ **Day 7** ᑌᑌ

Try that piece there. Okay, now try it here. Wow. We got a corner piece in. Good going. We're getting there.

Prayer: *Help me open my heart. Show me that love is real. Send me exactly what I need, when I need it. Help me trust that you are already showing me love every moment.*

The Twelve Steps of Alcoholics Anonymous*

1. We admitted we were powerless over alcohol—that our lives had become unmanageable.

2. Came to believe that a Power greater than ourselves could restore us to sanity.

3. Made a decision to turn our will and our lives over to the care of God *as we understood Him.*

4. Made a searching and fearless moral inventory of ourselves.

5. Admitted to God, to ourselves, and to another human being the exact nature of our wrongs.

6. Were entirely ready to have God remove all these defects of character.

7. Humbly asked Him to remove our shortcomings.

8. Made a list of all persons we had harmed, and became willing to make amends to them all.

9. Made direct amends to such people wherever possible, except when to do so would injure them or others.

10. Continued to take personal inventory and when we were wrong promptly admitted it.

11. Sought through prayer and meditation to improve our conscious contact with God *as we understood Him,* praying only for knowledge of His will for us and the power to carry that out.

12. Having had a spiritual awakening as the result of these steps, we tried to carry this message to alcoholics, and to practice these principles in all our affairs.

---

* The Twelve Steps of AA are taken from *Alcoholics Anonymous,* 4th ed., published by AA World Services, Inc., New York, N.Y., 59-60. Reprinted with permission of AA World Services, Inc. (See editor's note on copyright page.)

About the Author

Melody Beattie is the author of numerous best-selling books, including *Codependent No More* and *The Language of Letting Go.* She lives in Malibu, California.